Conciliation in industrial disputes

International Labour Office   Geneva

ISBN 92-2-101007-4

First published 1973

PRINTED BY C.A.G.S.A. - AVDA. JOSE ANTONIO, 719, BARCELONA-13

CONTENTS

	Page
Introduction	1
1. An over-all view of conciliation	3
Conciliation and collective bargaining	4
Conciliation and arbitration	5
Conciliation by an individual or by a board	6
Selection of conciliators	7
Voluntary and compulsory conciliation	8
The government conciliation service	9
Location of the service	9
Individual conciliators	10
Conciliation boards	11
2. General background of conciliation	13
Industrial disputes	13
Interest disputes	14
Grievance disputes	15
Disputes over unfair labour practices	16
Recognition disputes	17
Experience of collective labour relations	17
Systems of collective bargaining	18
Importance given to conciliation and arbitration respectively	20
3. The conciliator's qualifications	23
Personal qualities	23
Independence and impartiality	24
Commitment	24
Other personal qualities	27
Professional qualifications	28
Knowledge of industry and of the industrial relations system	28
Ability to profit from experience and research	29

Page

4. **The conciliator's preparations** 31

Pre-dispute readiness 31
   Desirability of information services 31
   Background information required 32
      (a) On employers and trade unions 32
      (b) On agreements, awards and wage orders 32
      (c) On past negotiations and disputes between particular parties . 33
      (d) On current developments and trends 34
Specific case preparation 35
   Case folder 36
   Information to be collected 36
      (a) On the background and facts of the dispute 36
      (b) On the issues 37
      (c) On personalities 37

5. **The conciliator's entry into a dispute** 39

Initiation of conciliation procedure 39
   Timing 39
   Assignment of cases 41
Preliminary contacts with the parties 42
   Giving information 43
   Obtaining information 44
   Establishing working relations 45

6. **Types of meetings and arrangements for them** 47

Types of meetings 47
   Joint conferences 47
   Separate meetings 49
   Private meetings 51
   Choice and sequence 53
Arrangements and preparations 54
   Place of meeting 54
   Accommodation 54
   Invitation to meetings 55
   Number and powers of representatives 55
   Production of documents 56
   Conciliator's case preparation for individual meetings 56

7. **Conduct of meetings** 59

Joint conferences 60
   Greetings and preliminary discussions 60
   Introductions and seating 61
   Opening statements and presentation of cases 61
   Chairmanship 64

Page

Separate meetings 65
   The call for separate meetings 66
   Atmosphere and procedure 67
Questions concerning both kinds of meeting 68
   Record of proceedings 69
   Order of discussion of the issues 69
   Duration of meetings 70
   Adjournment 70
   Press statements 71

8. The sequential pattern of conciliation 75

Hard posture 77
Search for accommodation 78
   Attitude of inquiry 78
   Evaluation and presentation of alternatives 79
   Conciliation of intra-party differences 81
Mood for settlement 83

9. Conciliation techniques 85

Conciliation as an art 85
   Personal style 85
   Listening, asking questions and timing 86
   Persuasion 87
     (a) Understanding the parties 87
     (b) Moral authority of the conciliator 88
     (c) Marshalling pressures 88
The many sides of the conciliator 91
   Discussion leader 92
   Alternative target or safety valve 92
   Communication link 93
   Prober 93
   Source of information and ideas 93
   Sounding board 93
   Protector 94
   Fail-safe device 94
   Stimulator 94
   Sympathiser 94
   Assessor or adviser 95
   Advocate 95
   Face-saver 96
   Coach or trainer 96
Proposals and counter-proposals 97
   By the parties 97
   By the conciliator 99

Page

10. Situations admitting of little compromise 101

Disputes over trade union rights and workers' grievances 101
    Unfair labour practices 102
    Recognition disputes 103
    Grievance disputes 104
        (a) "Yes or No" cases 104
        (b) Disciplinary action 105
        (c) Application and interpretation of collective agreements . . 105
        (d) Law enforcement and conciliation 106
        (e) Grievances and contract negotiations 107
Strike and lockout situations 108
    On-going strikes and lockouts 108
    Threatened strikes and lockouts 109

11. Conclusion of conciliation proceedings, and subsequent action . . . 113

Drafting of agreement, if any 113
Failure to reach agreement 114
Conciliation reports 115
Subsequent action 116
    Informal procedures 116
        (a) Workers' ballot 116
        (b) Reference to a senior conciliator 117
    Formal procedures 117
        (a) Conciliation boards 118
        (b) Fact-finding 118
        (c) Voluntary arbitration 119

12. Preventive conciliation 121

Post-conciliation preventive action 122
    Problems dealt with 123
    Procedures and methods of action 124
Promotional activities 125
    Specific objectives 126
    Advice and assistance 127
    Collection and dissemination of information 128
    Educational and training programmes 129

Appendix: Advice for conciliators 131

Basic attitude and approach 131
Meetings 131
The search for agreement 132

INTRODUCTION

This guide has been prepared mainly with a view to helping developing countries in their efforts to promote the orderly settlement of industrial disputes, with a minimum of work stoppages and other forms of disruption of production, and particularly to improve the performance of government conciliation officers.

In most countries the law prescribes that industrial disputes must be submitted to conciliation, but usually it does not specify how conciliation is to be carried out. The present guide constitutes an attempt to fill this gap by suggesting forms of behaviour, approaches and attitudes that will enable persons called upon to act as conciliators to carry out their functions more effectively, and thus with more success.

There are people who maintain that conciliation is an art ; that it is a natural talent which people do or do not possess ; and that therefore conciliaton cannot be learnt, particularly since every case that comes up is different from the next. While it is certainly true that some people are especially gifted for conciliation, there can be no doubt that young or inexperienced conciliators can learn much about attitudes and techniques from their more experienced colleagues. Such attitudes and techniques are the essential subject of this book.

It is specifically intended to serve a twofold purpose, namely to provide teaching material for basic training courses for newly appointed conciliators, and to serve as a guide for conciliators who have not had previous training.

While it is addressed to "conciliators", it is to be understood that this guide is concerned with people who are entrusted with the task of conciliation of industrial disputes, irrespective of their titles or main functions. It should thus meet the needs not only of professional or full-time conciliators but also of such persons as industrial relations officers, labour officers or labour inspectors, if conciliation is among their duties.

1

The guide is intended to be of use for conciliators working in different countries and under different national conditions, wherever open disagreement between employers and workers is conceivable under the existing labour relations system and wherever accommodation between the parties by way of conciliation is foreseen. It is not, however, a comparative study of law and practice regarding conciliation arrangements in different countries, but deals only with the question of how to equip conciliators to do their job more effectively.

The International Labour Office has prepared this guide with the assistance of two external collaborators from countries with a relatively long and varied experience in the operation of government conciliation services, namely Mr. Thomas Claro, C.B.E., M.V.O., former Chief Conciliation Officer, Ministry of Labour[1], United Kingdom ; and Mr. L. Lawrence Schultz, Director, Office of Planning and Development, Federal Mediation and Conciliation Service, United States.

The book is based on their contributions as well as on ILO sources. The latter include the results of ILO regional seminars in the field of labour relations, the work of ILO labour relations experts sent to a number of developing countries and other information available to the ILO regarding the situation in developing countries. Among the seminars just referred to, particular mention may be made of an Asian regional seminar on the prevention and settlement of industrial disputes, held in Kuala Lumpur in December 1961, and an African regional seminar for English-speaking countries on conciliation and arbitration of industrial disputes, held in Kampala in November 1962.[2]

Special efforts have been made in the preparation of the guide to take account of the conditions that generally prevail in developing countries and that affect the conciliation of industrial disputes. However, for use both as training material and as a guide for conciliators, the suggestions made in these pages will need to be adjusted to the particular circumstances of individual developing countries.

The final draft of the guide was prepared by Mr. Eladio Daya, of the Labour Law and Labour Relations Branch of the International Labour Office.

---

[1] Now Department of Employment.

[2] See ILO Labour-Management Relations Series : No. 15, *Prevention and settlement of industrial disputes in Asia*, Documents submitted to and report of an Asian regional seminar ... (Geneva, 1962, mimeographer) ; and No. 37, *Conciliation and arbitration of industrial disputes in English-speaking countries in Africa*, Record of proceedings of, and contributions submitted to, an African regional seminar ... (Geneva, 1970).

AN OVER-ALL VIEW OF CONCILIATION

1

Conciliation[1] is a process of peace-making. As a human institution, it is probably as old as man's interest in the peaceful resolution of conflicts. It has certainly been used since time immemorial to settle disputes and adjust differences between private persons. It has been most usefully employed to smooth out serious disagreements which threaten the rupture of established relationships, such as those between husbands and wives, among associates and friends, and among partners in common endeavours.

Conciliation and mediation, together with good offices, have always been important in the field of international relations for the peaceful settlement of conflicts between States and for the maintenance of international peace. In the world today there is probably only one other field where conciliation or mediation is of comparable importance for nations and the human community: the field of industrial relations. It is, moreover, in this field that this method of

---

[1] For the purpose of this guide, "conciliation" and "mediation" are regarded as equivalent terms referring to essentially the same kind of third-party intervention in promoting the voluntary settlement of disputes. On a strict interpretation of their etymological origins a distinction might be drawn between the two terms. (Conciliation would be limited to encouraging the parties to discuss their differences and to helping them develop their own proposed solutions. Mediation, on the other hand, would imply a stronger form of intervention, and a mediator would be permitted to offer to the parties proposals for settlement.) The distinction between the two terms has tended to disappear in industrial relations practice, and there is no consistency in their use from one country to another : in many countries either "conciliation" or "mediation" is used, or both terms are employed interchangeably, to denote the same process of third-party intervention ; in a number of other countries the two terms are employed to designate different forms of third-party intervention in promoting voluntary settlement. For the sake of simplicity only the words "conciliation" and "conciliator" will be used throughout this guide, on the understanding that they are interchangeable with "mediation" and "mediator" where in accordance with national practice those are the terms employed or in vogue. It may be noted in this connection that the expression "good offices", which denotes a milder form of third-party intervention than either conciliation or mediation, has not gained currency in the lexicon of industrial relations, but the idea of "good offices" is implicit in the concept of conciliation in the settlement of industrial disputes.

settling disputes has been most frequently and intensively used and has thus achieved the highest degree of development and refinement.

Conciliation may be described as the practice by which the services of a neutral third party are used in a dispute as a means of helping the disputing parties to reduce the extent of their differences and to arrive at an amicable settlement or agreed solution. It is a process of rational and orderly discussion of differences between the parties to a dispute under the guidance of the conciliator.

As a process of peace-making in industrial relations, conciliation aims to bring about the speedy settlement of disputes without resort to strikes or lockouts, and to hasten the termination of work stoppages when these have occurred. The steps that a conciliator may take to bring about an amicable settlement vary from one country to another, but always his function is to assist the parties towards a mutually acceptable compromise or solution. For this the only powers on which he can really rely are his powers of reasoning and persuasion.

A unique and essential characteristic of the conciliation process is its flexibility, which sets it apart from other methods of settling industrial disputes.[1] A conciliator cannot follow the same procedure in every case ; he must adjust his approaches, strategy and techniques to the circumstances of each dispute. Probably for this reason it has sometimes been said that conciliation is an art ; the "conciliator is a solitary artist recognising at most a few guiding stars and depending mainly on his personal power of divination".[2]

CONCILIATION AND COLLECTIVE BARGAINING

The practice of conciliation in industrial disputes has developed mainly in connection with disputes arising from the failure of collective bargaining, i.e. the negotiations between the parties with a view to the conclusion of a collective agreement. Conciliation has thus been described as an extension of collective bargaining with third-party assistance, or simply as "assisted collective bargaining".

The representatives of the parties in collective bargaining will usually also be their representatives at the conciliation proceedings. On the two sides, at

---

[1] Various terms, such as "industrial dispute", "labour dispute" or "trade dispute" are used in national practice to identify the differences between employers and workers. In this guide those terms are regarded as equivalent, but for the sake of simplicity only the expression "industrial dispute" will be used. For the various types of industrial disputes see Chapter 2.

[2] Arthur Meyer : "Function of the mediator in collective bargaining", in *Industrial and Labor Relations Review* (New York State School of Industrial and Labor Relations), Vol. 13, No. 2, p. 159.

the bilateral negotiation stage, these representatives constitute each party's "negotiating committee". At the conciliation stage the parties continue to have their negotiating committees. It is therefore also usual to speak of the joint discussions between the parties in conciliation proceedings as negotiations.

The voluntary settlement which is the aim of conciliation is nothing more nor less than the parties' reaching an agreement, which is as much a collective bargaining agreement as one resulting from unaided, direct negotiations between the parties. Viewed from another angle, collective bargaining is a process of joint decision making. Essentially the same process is involved in conciliation, and although the conciliator participates in it, the joint decision which is aimed at is one made by the parties themselves. The view of collective bargaining as a process of joint decision making makes it easier to understand the dynamics and complexity of conciliation, especially the many facets of the face-to-face relationships between the parties' negotiators as well as within each party's negotiating committee.

CONCILIATION AND ARBITRATION

The distinction between conciliation and arbitration in the settlement of industrial disputes is generally well established in national laws and regulations. However, when industrial relations are only in their infancy there may be a tendency to confuse the two processes, and the parties to a dispute may think of the person acting as conciliator between them as being empowered to lay down terms of settlement which they must accept. The point of the greatest practical importance in such a situation is that the conciliator himself should have a clear understanding of his role and should not make the mistake of assuming the role and authority of an arbitrator.

By his decision or award, an arbitrator has the power to determine a dispute submitted to him. In industrial disputes he may aim to make an award which he considers would be mutually acceptable to the parties, but he none the less substitutes his judgement for that of the parties with regard to the terms on which the dispute should be settled. It is not, however, the function of a conciliator to substitute his judgement for that of the parties with regard to the desirable terms of settlement. He may suggest possible lines of solution, or himself propose terms of settlement if such a course is in accordance with national practice ; but it is for the parties to accept or not to accept his suggestions or proposals : he cannot impose the terms of settlement upon them.

It is also important to note that the functions of conciliation and arbitration are not performed in the same way. An arbitrator usually conducts

5

a hearing of the parties and makes his award or decision afterwards. Arbitration proceedings do not necessarily follow the formal course of judicial proceedings, and arbitrators are not often bound by the technical rules of evidence observed by ordinary courts. Even, however, when allowance is made for this, conciliation proceedings are less formal, or more informal, than arbitration proceedings. While arbitration proceedings require the presence of both parties, the holding of a joint meeting is only one of the ways in which a conciliator performs his tasks.

CONCILIATION BY AN INDIVIDUAL OR BY A BOARD

In the preceding pages the word "conciliator" has been generally used to mean the neutral third party assisting in the voluntary settlement of disputes. Under the practice in a large number of countries this third party is very often a government official functioning as a conciliator in an individual capacity. In fact the methods and techniques of conciliation in industrial disputes have been largely developed on the basis of the experiences of individual conciliators ; it has indeed been often pointed out that conciliation is essentially a one-man job.

Conciliation may also be undertaken by a body consisting of several members, variously called a board, a council or a committee of conciliation and simply referred to in this guide as a conciliation board. It generally consists of an independent chairman together with employers' and workers' members, and it is the board as a whole which is usually given the task of promoting the settlement of a dispute referred to it. The procedure of a conciliation board is more formal than that followed by an individual conciliator, and the two procedures also differ in other respects.

Notwithstanding these differences there is an essential similarity in the conciliation process as carried out by an individual conciliator and by a board. In the case of a conciliation board, the work of conciliation devolves mainly on the chairman, who really functions on the board as the neutral third party. In performing his task he may use the methods and techniques of an individual conciliator, although the manner in which he does so will vary according to the role of the employers' and workers' members.

In one situation the ordinary members have a direct interest in the dispute and sit as the parties' representatives on the board. They will therefore be in the same position as the parties' negotiating committees in proceedings before an individual conciliator. The role of the chairman will thus be essentially the same as that of a conciliator functioning in an individual capacity. In another situation the employers' and workers' members are not directly connected with the dispute and are supposed to play a more objective role. They may assist the chairman in his neutral, third-party role—as a line of communication between him and the parties—in obtaining a realistic assessment of the parties' position, in formulating compromise solutions. Even in these cases, however, it will be difficult for the employers' and workers' members to be as completely objective as the chairman himself, and one of his main tasks will often be to reconcile the divergent positions of the employers' and workers' members.

SELECTION OF CONCILIATORS

Conciliation is now generally provided by governments but may also be instituted under private arrangements which are encouraged by governments in a number of countries. It is interesting to note that when conciliation was first used to settle industrial disputes the arrangements were made privately. Those were cases in which the parties to a dispute agreed to appoint a conciliator of their choice to help them in settling it, especially by presiding over their joint discussions. The person appointed as conciliator was usually an eminent one, jointly chosen by the parties for his prestige and personal qualifications, and therefore having their trust and confidence. Even with the development of government conciliation services, it is still possible in various countries for the parties to a dispute to agree to use a private conciliator.

At present, however, private arrangements for conciliation in industrial disputes are more generally made by agreement between employers' associations and trade unions.[1] The arrangements often also provide for arbitration, and involve the setting up of joint conciliation and arbitration machinery by the parties to the agreement. Various ways of using the services of a neutral third party in the agreed machinery have been developed. In most cases disputes are referred to the agreed machinery after failure of direct negotiations between the parties. This is not always the case, however, and an impartial chairman may take part in the negotiations from the beginning. In many cases disputes not settled through the agreed machinery may be referred to the government conciliation machinery.

As regards conciliation under government auspices, the International Labour Conference adopted in 1951 a Recommendation (No. 92) concerning voluntary conciliation and arbitration. It provides, in particular, that "volun-

---

[1] In certain countries the legal definition of the term "trade union" or "industrial association" includes both workers' and employers' organisations. In this guide "trade union" is used to refer only to workers' organisations, while organisations of employers are identified as "employers' associations" or "employers' organisations".

tary conciliation machinery, appropriate to national conditions, should be made available to assist in the prevention and settlement of disputes between employers and workers" and that "the procedure should be free of charge and expeditious". Conciliation under government auspices is generally governed by legislation concerning industrial relations or industrial disputes ; but national practice varies in regard to the arrangements by which the government provides conciliation. This question is discussed further below.

VOLUNTARY AND COMPULSORY CONCILIATION

Although the aim of conciliation is always an amicable settlement between the parties, in a number of countries conciliation arranged by the government has certain compulsory features : the procedure may be made compulsory by provisions requiring the parties' attendance at conciliation proceedings or empowering the conciliation authority to compel their attendance at such proceedings, as well as by the prohibition of strikes and lockouts without prior resort to conciliation.

In countries where conciliation is on an entirely voluntary basis conciliation may be offered to the parties if they have not requested it, but they are left entirely free to accept or not to accept the invitation. According to this conception, if the parties do not wish to accept the proffered conciliation, it will be useless to compel them to go through with the procedure. In the words of an English proverb, "You can lead a horse to water, but you cannot make it drink." On the other hand there will be no difficulty if the parties have faith in the competence of the government conciliation service, and if this condition is met they will willingly seek or welcome its assistance. It should accordingly be the task of the government conciliation service to satisfy this condition, and it should aim at gaining moral authority in the minds of its potential users.

In other quarters it is considered that compulsory conciliation can serve a useful purpose even if the parties' attitudes make the possibility of a voluntary settlement very unlikely. This view is advanced with particular force in regard to developing countries where management and trade unions may as yet have relatively little experience of collective labour relations. Very often the parties would hardly agree even to meet each other for direct negotiations; the management may refuse to recognise and have any dealings with the trade union. In such a situation the compulsory attendance of the parties at a conciliation meeting will help them to make each other's acquaintance and to become used to joint discussions. In other words, compulsory conciliation can serve as a means of educating, training and guiding the parties with regard to the nature and conduct of bilateral negotiations.

THE GOVERNMENT CONCILIATION SERVICE

Conciliation is generally provided by the government through an administrative unit which may have one of a variety of names. The size of the unit varies from country to country. In a large number of countries it also performs other, related functions in the field of industrial relations. This development has taken place not only in industrially advanced countries with relatively long experience of industrial relations but also in an increasing number of developing countries.

With industrialisation and the development of trade unions and collective bargaining the problems of industrial relations have become increasingly complex and difficult, and the objective of industrial peace has been seen to require more than an approach based mainly on methods of settling disputes and regulations to prevent strikes and lockouts. It is considered that progress towards that objective can be facilitated by a more positive approach that involves a variety of functions and methods of action requiring the services of specialised staff. The need for this kind of approach has been especially felt in countries where industrial relations policy aims at encouraging dialogue between employers and workers in resolving their problems.

The scope of the functions of the administrative unit concerned is often reflected by the words "industrial relations" or "labour relations" in its official designation. It may have responsibility for certain proceedings other than conciliation ; more generally it is given mainly promotional or advisory functions. It may, for example, encourage and advise on the establishment of agreed machinery and procedures, whether for the negotiation of collective agreements, the adjustment of grievances or the settlement of disputes ; advise on ways of eliminating or minimising the causes of disputes, grievances and friction, and on personnel policies and practices; promote consultation and co-operation between employers and workers and their organisations, and advise on the establishment of appropriate machinery for the purpose ; and encourage and assist in industrial relations training programmes for management and trade union personnel. For the purposes of this guide, the whole of this administrative unit will be covered by the generic term "government conciliation service".

Location of the service

In most countries the government conciliation service is part of the ministry or department of labour. In a number of these countries the minister or commissioner of labour is specifically designated by law as the authority responsible for conciliation. In other countries the law itself establishes a unit, which is made specially responsible for conciliation and related functions, within the ministry or department.

Under another system the conciliation authority is an autonomous organ, either completely independent of the ministry of labour or linked to it for administrative or budgetary purposes only. In many cases the organ in question is a board or commission composed of independent members only or including representatives of employers and workers. In yet another situation conciliation is a function of both the ministry of labour and an autonomous agency, ministry officials being generally responsible for initial intervention in disputes.

In general, the location of the conciliation service will be dictated by practical considerations. Where an organ is responsible for both conciliation and arbitration, or is vested with quasi-judicial functions, it appears to be the general practice to give it an autonomous status. What may be of real importance is that, whether the conciliation service is located within or outside the ministry of labour, it should be able to function without interference and with the largest possible degree of impartiality between employers and workers.

The traditional function of the ministry of labour to protect workers has sometimes been urged as a reason for giving the conciliation service autonomous status, on the assumption that the atmosphere of labour protection within the ministry would not be conducive to impartiality in disputes which oppose workers' interests to those of employers. In many countries where the ministry of labour is responsible for conciliation the government has sought to overcome this possible difficulty by setting up a conciliation service distinct and separate from the units responsible for law enforcement and labour inspection.

Individual conciliators

In a large number of countries the work of the conciliation service is mainly carried out by permanent officials functioning as individual conciliators. These officials are of three main kinds : *(a)* those who devote all their working time to conciliation and probably other industrial relations duties, and are officially designated as conciliators or as conciliation or industrial relations officers ; *(b)* officials who perform conciliation on a part-time basis and as one of their normal day-to-day functions ; and *(c)* officials at the higher executive or administrative levels who intervene in disputes on an ad hoc basis.

Officials who carry out conciliation as a part-time duty are usually labour inspectors or labour officers mainly engaged in the enforcement of labour laws. It has been argued that the performance by labour inspectors of conciliation and arbitration functions will be incompatible with, and will consequently hamper them in, the performance of their primary duties.[1] In this connection the Labour Inspection Recommendation, 1947 (No. 81), provides that "the functions of labour inspectors should not include that of acting as conciliator or arbitrator in proceedings concerning labour disputes".[2]

In many developing countries the function of conciliation was initially entrusted to labour inspectors, at a time when trade unions and collective bargaining were just beginning to develop and when disputes arose mainly from the claims or demands of individual workers or groups of workers. In recent years a growing number of those countries have adopted the practice of appointing full-time conciliation or industrial relations officers, although labour inspectors or labour officers may continue to deal with individual disputes or disputes of lesser importance.

In addition to permanent officials who are normally called upon to act as conciliators in their capacity as conciliation officers, industrial relations officers, labour officers or labour inspectors, it is not unusual in many countries for senior officials of the ministry or department of labour, such as commissioners and deputy commissioners of labour, to intervene as conciliators in major disputes. In some countries ministers of labour often intervene in disputes of national importance, especially those involving work stoppages. Cases in which heads of governments intervene in such disputes are not rare.

Government officials and members of government are not the only persons called upon to act as individual conciliators. In some countries the conciliation service is given the possibility of appointing private persons to serve as conciliators at government expense. The individuals so appointed are generally persons of knowledge and experience, such as university professors who have maintained close contacts with industry, retired officials of the ministry of labour, or well known professional men and civic leaders.

Conciliation boards

In certain countries the governments do not utilise the services of individual conciliators but provide for conciliation boards which include employers' and workers' members and are either set up as permanent bodies or constituted on an ad hoc basis. In a number of countries both conciliation boards and individual conciliators are used, and in practice a dispute is normally referred to a board only after an individual conciliator has failed to bring about a settlement.

---

[1] ILO: *Record of proceedings*, International Labour Conference, 30th Session, Geneva, 1947, p 510.
[2] Paragraph 8.

In cases where conciliation boards are constituted on an ad hoc basis the employers' and workers' members are usually nominated by the parties to the dispute in respect of which the board has been set up. On the other hand, where the boards are established as permanent bodies, the usual practice is for the employers' and workers' members to be nominated or selected by employers' and workers' organisations. These two methods may be combined in a system under which the competent authority appoints a panel or panels of potential members nominated by employers' and workers' organisations, from which the parties to a dispute select the individuals to be members of the board dealing with that dispute.

A conciliation board is usually empowered to investigate or inquire into the facts of the dispute, and the employers' and workers' members perform an important role in the appreciation or assessment of the facts. As indicated earlier, however, the main task of conciliation normally devolves upon the independent chairman, who performs it by presiding over the conciliation meetings and in other ways. Very often the chairman is a government official—a representative of the ministry of labour or the competent labour inspector.

THE INDUSTRIAL BACKGROUND 2

The conciliation of industrial disputes is affected by two sets of conditions. There are, on the one hand, the objective conditions—factors external to the conciliator—which affect the work of conciliation in general ; and on the other hand, the subjective conditions, which relate to the conciliator himself and his individual performance.

The objective conditions, with which this chapter is concerned, include the nature of the issues involved in industrial disputes, and a wide variety of other factors that form part of the general background of conciliation, such as local experience of collective labour relations, the prevailing system of collective bargaining and the importance accorded to conciliation in the national system of settling disputes.

INDUSTRIAL DISPUTES

In general, the government conciliation service would be competent to intervene in disputes between employers and workers which come under the legal definition of "industrial dispute" (or "labour dispute" or "trade dispute", as the case may be). In dealing with a particular dispute, however, a conciliator has to adjust his approach to the nature of the issues involved; the nature of the issues will in particular affect the extent to which the dispute is amenable to compromise solutions. In a number of countries the law itself distinguishes between various types of disputes, essentially on the basis of the nature of the issues involved, and lays down different settlement procedures or includes other special provisions with regard to particular types of controversies between employers and workers.

Under the most common practice the distinction is made between two main types of disputes relating to terms of employment. They are : *(a)* disputes that arise out of deadlocks in the negotiations for a collective agreement, subsequently simply referred to in this guide as "interest disputes"; and *(b)* disputes that arise from day-to-day workers' grievances or complaints, subsequently simply referred to as "grievance disputes". In addition, in various countries special provisions apply to two other types of disputes relating to organisational rights, namely *(c)* those arising from acts of interference with the exercise of the right to organise, or acts commonly known in the countries concerned as "unfair labour practices"; and *(d)* disputes over the right of a trade union to represent a particular class or category of workers for purposes of collective bargaining, simply referred to here as "recognition disputes".

Interest disputes

These disputes are also described as "conflicts of interest" or "economic disputes"; they generally correspond to what in certain countries are called "collective labour disputes". National practice is not uniform in its identification of this type of dispute, but the essential elements are more or less the same : in general they relate to the establishment of new terms and conditions of employment for the general body of workers concerned. In most cases the disputes originate from trade union demands or proposals for job security, wage increases, fringe benefits, or other improvements in the terms of employment.[1] These demands or proposals are normally made with a view to the conclusion of a collective agreement, and a dispute arises when the parties fail in their negotiations to reach an agreement. The conciliation of this type of dispute is itself a part of the collective bargaining process, being an extension or a continuation of the negotiations between the parties, with the conciliator's assistance.

The expressions "conflict of interests" and "economic disputes" both describe the nature of the issues involved. The negotiations over these issues are usually a matter of give-and-take, of haggling and bargaining, between the parties. The practices prevailing in other sectors of the economy may provide some guidance on possible lines of accommodation. Apart from this the parties cannot refer to any definite mutually binding standards ; each side seeks to obtain for itself the best bargain it can under the existing market and economic conditions. If the parties can resort to a strike or lockout, they will be influenced in maintaining their positions by their estimates of each other's bargaining power. In brief, to a much greater extent than in the case of other types of disputes, the issues in interest disputes are "compromisable" and therefore lend themselves best to conciliation.

---

[1] However, collective bargaining may take place through other forms of workers' representation.

Grievance disputes

Grievance disputes are also variously called "conflicts of rights" or "legal" disputes. They involve individual workers only or a group of workers in the same situation, and correspond largely to what in certain countries are called "individual" disputes. As previously indicated, they generally arise from day-to-day relations in the undertaking, usually as a protest by the worker or workers concerned against an act of the management. Probably one of the most common causes of grievances is the dismissal of a worker, which he or his union considers to be unjustified. In some countries grievances arise especially over the interpretation and application of collective agreements, and grievance disputes are therefore also called "interpretation" disputes. There is, however, a great deal of variation in national practice with regard to the kinds of differences between employers and workers that would fall within this category of disputes.

In the Examination of Grievances Recommendation (No. 130), which it adopted in 1967, the International Labour Conference took account of this wide variety of national practices, and under the Recommendation "the grounds for a grievance may be any measure or situation which concerns the relations between employer and worker or which affects or may affect the conditions of employment of one or several workers in the undertaking when that measure or situation appears contrary to provisions of an applicable collective agreement or an individual contract of employment, to works rules, to laws or regulations or to the custom or usage of the occupation, branch of economic activity or country, regard being had to principles of good faith".[1]

The expressions "conflicts of rights" and "legal disputes" describe the nature of the issues involved. Workers' grievances are generally based on an alleged violation of an existing right, or on alleged unfair treatment by the management, as judged by certain rules. In contrast to interest disputes, there is some more or less definite standard for settling a grievance dispute—the relevant provision of the collective agreement, employment contract, works rules or law, or custom or usage. The main issue relates to the interpretation and application of the provision, custom or usage; it invariably requires an ascertainment and appreciation of the facts and, where the grievance is based on a contractual or conventional right, a determination of the intentions of the parties to the agreement that is involved, at the time when the agreement was concluded.

---

[1] Paragraph 3. The Recommendation deals with the establishment of grievance procedures within the undertaking for the speedy and equitable settlement of grievances. Under Paragraph 4, the provisions of the Recommendation are not applicable to collective claims aimed at the modification of terms and conditions of employment (and which may give rise to interest disputes).

These issues are more or less like those in cases before the ordinary courts. In many countries labour courts or tribunals have been set up to adjudicate on grievance disputes or "legal" or "individual" disputes. In many others the government promotes voluntary arbitration for their settlement. Hence in a good number of these countries grievance disputes do not come before government conciliators.

Disputes over unfair labour practices

The most common "unfair labour practices", in industrial relations parlance, are attempts by the management of an undertaking to discriminate against workers for being trade union members or for trade union activity. In most cases the objects of such discriminatory treatment are trade union officials or representatives employed in the undertaking, and trade unionists who have actively participated in a strike. These unfair labour practices are also known in various countries as "trade union victimisation".

In certain countries the law has established a special procedure for the prevention of unfair labour practices, generally including the possibility of reinstatement of dismissed workers; such a procedure obviates or precludes conciliation. In the absence of such a procedure unfair labour practices will be subject to the normal procedures for settling disputes if they fall within the definition of an "industrial dispute". This is generally the case when the unfair labour practice consists of dismissal. The usual demand is for the reinstatement of the dismissed worker.

Although, for this reason, the dispute relates to employment and can be said to belong to the category of grievance disputes, the issue differs essentially from that in other forms of workers' grievances or other cases of dismissal based on the workers' misconduct. The dismissal in a case of unfair labour practice is a symptom of a more deep-seated cause, namely a negative attitude on the part of the management towards trade unionism and the employees' right to form or join a trade union. Any attempt to settle the dispute by way of conciliation will need to be directed to this problem of the employer's attitude.

In certain countries unfair labour practices, especially those involving dismissals, are criminal offences. That may be helpful in any effort, short of the institution of criminal proceedings, to induce a change in the management attitude. Apart from this, and as in the case of grievance disputes, the process of settlement would require an inquiry into the facts—whether in fact the worker has been dismissed for being an active trade unionist.

Recognition disputes

This type of dispute arises when the management of an undertaking or an employers' organisation refuses to recognise a trade union for purposes of collective bargaining.[1] As in the case of unfair labour practices, in a number of countries a special procedure for settling recognition disputes has been established and these disputes do not normally come before the government conciliation service. In most other countries the service is usually competent to intervene in this type of dispute ; but in certain countries recognition disputes may not come within the scope of the legislative definition of an industrial dispute.[2] Even so, government conciliators in these countries may have to intervene, at least on an informal basis, in a dispute of this kind, especially when it is likely to lead to a strike.

Issues in recognition disputes will differ according to the cause which has led the management to refuse recognition. It may be that the management dislikes trade unionism and will not have anything to do with a trade union : the problem is then one of attitude, as in the case of trade union victimisation referred to earlier. However, the management's refusal may be on the ground that the union requesting recognition is not sufficiently representative, or that there are several unions in the undertaking making conflicting claims to recognition. In this case the resolution of the issue may depend on the existence or non-existence of rules for determining the representative capacity of trade unions for the purpose of collective bargaining. Such rules need not necessarily be laid down by law : they may be conventional or derived from prevailing practices in the country ; in various countries rules for trade union recognition have been laid down in voluntary codes of principles or industrial relations charters agreed to by employers' and workers' organisations.

EXPERIENCE OF COLLECTIVE LABOUR RELATIONS

Within a country the extent to which individual managers, trade unions and employers' associations have acquired the experience and habits of mutual dealings has quite important implications for the work of conciliators,

---

[1] Closely related to recognition disputes between employers and trade unions are the "jurisdictional" or "demarcation" disputes between trade unions that compete in organising the workers in a particular industry, trade or occupation. In general, the central workers' organisations prefer to deal with the latter disputes themselves, and government conciliators are not normally asked to intervene. They would, however, be competent to do so under a definition of industrial dispute which includes a difference among workers concerning employment.

[2] Where, for example, an industrial dispute is defined as a difference concerning employment or conditions of employment.

both as regards the performance of the conciliation function and as regards the types of disputes in which conciliators are normally called upon to intervene.

In the more economically advanced countries, where experience of collective labour relations has been relatively long, the disputes that come before conciliators, generally after the parties have had some thorough and extensive negotiations among themselves, are predominantly or exclusively interest disputes. The parties will be represented in the conciliation proceedings by experienced negotiators who will be able to rely on the assistance of the research services of their respective organisations. The negotiations before the conciliator tend to be marked by hard and tight bargaining; this makes the task of the conciliator in seeking possible fields for compromise a difficult one. On the other hand, he will not have much difficulty in presiding over the discussions, since the parties' negotiators will themselves be familiar with the course of such proceedings.

In the developing countries the situation is different. In some countries there is little or no collective bargaining, and most disputes arise from grievances. More generally, conciliators in developing countries have to deal with a large number of disputes between parties for whom collective labour relations constitute a relatively novel experience. Quite often disputes are brought to the conciliation service before the parties have had meaningful negotiations among themselves. A good proportion of the disputes will involve relatively uncomplicated issues which could easily have been disposed of by sufficiently experienced negotiators. Very often, a major difficulty for the conciliator is that the attitude of either party or both parties may prevent serious negotiations. One party may go through the motions of participating in the conciliation proceedings without any real intention of agreeing to a settlement. The parties' inexperience of bilateral negotiations may also be expected to give rise to procedural difficulties in joint meetings. They may tend to support their respective positions by generalisations or abstract reasoning rather than by concrete arguments and data. In this situation the role of the conciliator as chairman of joint meetings becomes of critical importance.

SYSTEMS OF COLLECTIVE BARGAINING

The approaches and methods of conciliators will be geared to the prevailing national system or pattern of collective bargaining which varies from country to country.

It has become usual to distinguish between two main methods of collective bargaining according to the level at which it is carried out. It may take place at the level of an industry or occupation (national or regional) usually between a trade union and an employers' association or sometimes a group of employers. Under the other method bargaining takes place at the level of an enterprise or plant, or a section of it, usually between a trade union or, in some countries, a works council, works committee or a similar body, and the management of the enterprise or plant.

The first method is often briefly described as industry-wide, occupation-wide or multi-employer bargaining, the second as plant-level or single-employer bargaining. While in certain countries the collective bargaining system may be based largely or exclusively on one of these methods, in other countries both methods are extensively employed, although their relative frequency may differ. It appears that in a large number of developing countries the trade unions are mostly formed at the level of individual undertakings and the prevailing system of collective bargaining is that carried out at that level, or involves only one employer.

The implications of these two methods of bargaining for conciliators are affected by such factors as the obvious differences in the strength of the parties involved, in their financial resources for research and in the identity of their negotiators. The union negotiators in industry-wide or occupation-wide bargaining will often be full-time union officials ; in plant-level bargaining they will be wholly or largely union officials employed in the undertaking. In countries with well developed trade union movements, a union involved in plant-level bargaining is generally a local unit of a national union, and in addition to the local union officials the union negotiators may include national, regional or district union representatives ; but in the situation frequently met with in many developing countries the union involved is a plant-level union which depends on its own resources for collective bargaining and undertakes this activity through officials employed in the undertaking.

National practice also varies with regard to the whole range of matters that are typically the subject of negotiations. However, in that respect it is possible to distinguish between two main types of bargaining. One may be described as the comprehensive type of bargaining, based on a detailed "charter of demands" or detailed contract proposals put forward by a union. The list of items may relate to employment, manning, wages and hours, overtime pay, paid holidays, paid sick leave, bonus payments, other fringe benefits, severance pay and so forth. In certain countries they also include such matters as union recognition, union security, union check-off, management rights, grievance procedures, union-management consultation and the so-called peace obligation. [1] Under the other type of bargaining the negotiations at any one

---

[1] This refers to a clause in a collective agreement under which the parties undertake not to resort to a strike or lockout except under the conditions specified in the agreement.

time cover a limited number of items, even only one or two, generally including wage questions. In comprehensive bargaining the issues are more complicated but there is more room for compromise, partly because the parties usually attach different priorities or degrees of importance to each of the disputed issues. In particular, where the parties are free to stage a strike or lockout before or during conciliation a trade union will go on strike, and an employer will be willing to risk a strike, on a particular issue but not on the others.

These two types of bargaining also have consequences for the frequency of negotiations and the likelihood of disputes. Under the comprehensive system of bargaining the parties usually specify in the collective agreement a period during which it shall remain in force. This period is usually not less than one year, and may be two or more, according to national practice. The agreement is supposed to represent a settlement of all pending issues between the parties, and to govern their relationship for that period. Under the more limited system of bargaining an agreement on certain items would not preclude further negotiations on other items. During a given period there may be a series of negotiations on number of separate matters.

IMPORTANCE GIVEN TO CONCILIATION AND ARBITRATION RESPECTIVELY

The conciliators' chances of bringing about amicable settlements are greatly affected by the possibility that a dispute will be referred to compulsory arbitration, either automatically or almost as a practical certainty, in the event of failure of conciliation. [1] National practice differs with regard to the disputes to which compulsory arbitration may be applied and the conditions under which it may be resorted to, but it is mainly in connection with interest disputes. It has been indicated earlier that in many countries adjudication is a preferred method of settling grievance disputes in which, in view of the nature of the issues involved, there is less room for compromise.

With regard to interest disputes conciliation is the principal means or may under normal conditions be the only available method of settlement under government auspices in certain countries. The importance given to conciliation is often reflected in the relatively high official status of government conciliators, which gives them a useful measure of moral authority and personal prestige. In such countries the pressures upon the parties to reach a settlement by conciliation are the same as in direct negotiations between them. In principle,

---

[1] Compulsory arbitration is taken here to mean the submission of a dispute to arbitration for final and binding settlement otherwise than by agreement or common consent of both parties, i.e. on application by only one party, or by government decision.

in case of disagreement, the parties are free to resort to a trial of strength, the results of which will determine the final terms of settlement. However, there is a strong inducement for the parties to explore fully every possibility of settlement in order to avoid a strike or lockout, which may be very costly, and somewhat uncertain in its outcome.

Where compulsory arbitration is available the task of the conciliator becomes more difficult. It is not only that there is not the above-mentioned inducement on the parties to reach a settlement ; compulsory arbitration may actually tend to produce an opposite result. Either side may think that it can obtain more favourable terms under an arbitration award, and is tempted to avoid a settlement by conciliation so that the dispute will be brought to arbitration. This temptation becomes greater if the conciliator can be brought before the arbitration tribunal to testify on what has transpired in the proceedings before him. During conciliation, this possibility can inhibit the parties from making counter-proposals which, if made known to the arbitration tribunal, can affect the terms of the award it will make. In the absence of a real spirit of give-and-take between the parties, conciliation tends to become a mere formality, a step on the way to compulsory arbitration.

THE CONCILIATOR'S QUALIFICATIONS

3

A basic aspect of the work of a conciliator is his personal relationship with the parties to disputes in which he is involved. In order to be effective he must have their trust and confidence.

It is very important to appreciate fully the position of the ordinary conciliator in this regard. We may compare his position with that of a private conciliator selected by the parties or that of a senior government official who occasionally acts as a conciliator in disputes. A private conciliator or a senior government official may not succeed in conciliating a particular dispute, but they enjoy advantages which make it likely that they will be effective in leading the parties to a settlement.

When the parties to a dispute agree to utilise the services of a private conciliator they select a person for his qualifications and experience, which they know well ; they choose him precisely because they both believe in his ability to help them. In conciliating a dispute a minister of labour or a senior government official does not have this advantage of having been selected by the parties. He has, however, his own wealth of experience, his personal prestige, and last but not least the authority of his office. These make his intervention generally welcome by the parties.

The ordinary conciliator does not enjoy these advantages. He is thrust by the government into a dispute, whether the parties like it or not. Unless they believe that he can be of real help to them, his efforts are almost always bound to fail. To be able to win their trust and confidence and to be effective in his work, a conciliator must possess certain personal qualities and qualifications. And, while he must prepare himself adequately in dealing with a specific case, he must be always prepared and ready to be called upon to intervene in any dispute at any time.

PERSONAL QUALITIES

It is perhaps difficult in describing the personal qualities which a conciliator should possess to avoid creating the impression that he must be a "superman". This is of course not the case, but there are certain basic characteristics essential to the work of conciliation which he should possess. Some of these characteristics are primarily a matter of attitude, which it would be inexcusable for a conciliator not to develop in himself. Some other characteristics are inborn traits which the average person possesses to a greater or lesser degree. A person may be exceptionally gifted with these traits and have a natural aptitude and talent for conciliation. The ordinary conciliator can be expected to possess some of these inborn traits. He should see it as his task to enhance them by conscious study and effort.

Independence and impartiality

Independence and impartiality are the two attributes which every conciliator should possess, regardless of other qualifications. It is essential that he should not only possess these qualities but be also clearly seen to possess them. To appear independent and impartial is no less important than actually to be so ; in this regard a conciliator must be above suspicion.

The moment that one party is led to suspect, by any word or gesture on his part, that he is biased in favour of the other party, he loses his value, because it is essential that both sides should have confidence in his integrity and neutrality. In developing countries there are usually differences in the social status or prestige of the parties' negotiators and in the strength of the organisations they represent. A conciliator should be independent enough not to be swayed or influenced by these factors. He should be able to resist undue pressures or persuasion from powerful employers or unions.

Through his handling of various cases a conciliator should be able to establish a reputation for himself, and make both sides of industry accept that he is a completely unbiased and reliable conciliator. Even a single incident in which his independence and impartiality becomes suspect to one party can adversely affect his reputation for a long time afterwards, and indeed he may never succeed in regaining it.

Commitment

Conciliation in certain cases means arduous work. A conciliator should be physically and psychologically fit for the rigours of his task. He has to do a certain amount of desk work, but his cases will require him to work outside the confines of an office. He does not have the same working day as most government servants, and conciliation meetings may last for hours on end. For this reason among others, a personal factor calling for particular emphasis is therefore the fundamental need for a conciliator to have a positive attitude towards his work. He must have a strong and deeply held conviction of the importance and usefulness of conciliation, and he must like or learn to like the work. As a public official a conciliator can easily allow himself to sink into the routine and the leisurely pace usually associated with government bureaucracy, but conciliation, if it is to be performed effectively, can never be a matter of bureaucratic routine.

Unfortunately, the conditions of employment of government conciliators in certain countries may be discouraging for them. They may think that their pay and other conditions of service are not commensurate with the importance of their function and responsibilities. Material inducement is probably as important for the motivation of a conciliator in performing his duties as it is in the case of other public servants; and it would be difficult to blame a conciliator for not doing his best if he feels that he is not sufficiently rewarded. Nevertheless, conciliation is fertile in non-material rewards which can be sources of boundless satisfaction for the person engaged in it. There are probably not many spheres of paid employment, whether in the government service or outside, where the work can provide greater personal satisfaction than in conciliation. It is quite important that a government conciliator should fully appreciate this advantage of his work.

It needs no emphasising that for developing countries industrial peace is essential for stable and accelerated economic growth. Government conciliators are in a very special position to contribute to the promotion and maintenance of industrial peace in their countries. They can play an effective role in preventing work stoppages and in bringing to an early termination such stoppages as may have occurred. It need hardly be said that in his work of industrial peacemaking a conciliator is rendering a vitally important service to his country. Nor need it be said that he should be deeply conscious of this and that it should give him tremendous satisfaction.

The fact cannot be overlooked that in a materialistic civilisation such as now encompasses the world there are probably increasing numbers of people for whom talk of service to one's country is pure romance or outmoded idealism ; and it may have become fashionable in certain circles to be cynical about the idea of service to one's country, or indifferent to it. While the adoption of any such attitude by a conciliator may not be wholly fatal to his usefulness, it deprives him of something which could make his work much more pleasant to perform.

Much more, of course, can be said about the importance, usefulness and special character of conciliation. It has been noted that conciliation "is an expression of one of the highest virtues which can be practised—the desire to understand and be just to one another. Each time that one attempts to resolve a conflict without force one renders to men an enormous service in leading them in the path of wisdom and of respect for themselves and for each other".[1] And while it has been noted earlier that a conciliator must like his work, there is really no need of special urging for him to do so ; the work is interesting enough, and a liking for it will come naturally to anyone who has some aptitude for conciliation and realises its potentialities.

One of the main causes of frustration and unhappiness among employed people is that they are engaged in work which is monotonous, repetitive or of a routine character and provides no scope for judgement and self-expression, for exciting adventure in creativity and ingenuity. In his work a conciliator is in the enviable position of exercising independent judgement and responsibility ; this is the natural aspiration of people who want to be able to show their worth, and is not the lot of many public servants. While he may receive guidance or assistance from the headquarters of the service or from his immediate superior, once he intervenes in a dispute he assumes full control of the proceedings.

Every dispute in which a conciliator intervenes is an opportunity for him to make a clearly identifiable contribution and to express his personality and his creative impulse. Subject to a few fundamental rules, he works according to his own lights, and he alone is responsible for the result. Each dispute is unique, and he can often find in a new dispute a fresh challenge to his inventiveness and powers of innovation. Even though he may not succeed in settling a dispute, he can be satisfied with the way he did his job.

What should be the attitude of a conciliator when he is dealing with a dispute which can afterwards be referred to arbitration, or in which the parties' attitudes make it seem to him that he is engaged in a hopeless or impossible task ? It is easy for a conciliator to give up in such a case and to make only a perfunctory or half-hearted effort at conciliation. But he can also take the view that the difficulties are a further challenge to his resourcefulness and imagination.

A conciliator should never allow conciliation proceedings before him to constitute a mere formality or a step on the road to arbitration, voluntary or compulsory. He must be able to offer to the parties inducements that will persuade them to prefer a settlement with his assistance and to make serious efforts to reach agreement. It may also need to be emphasised that in many developing countries the measure of the effectiveness of a conciliator cannot

---

[1] Paul-Henri Spaak, former Prime Minister and Minister of Foreign Affairs of Belgium, in foreword to Elmore Jackson : *Meeting of minds : A way to peace through mediation* (New York, McGraw-Hill, 1952).

be limited to his success in bringing about voluntary settlements, though this will always be his objective. For parties experiencing collective industrial relations for the first time, a conciliator can perform a very useful function by making the conciliation proceedings a worthwhile, instructive experience ; this possibility will be open to a conciliator not only in cases in which he can compel the parties' attendance but also those in which conciliation is voluntary. Whenever a conciliator succeeds in helping the parties to gain some skill in bilateral negotiations or in inducing some positive changes in their attitude, his efforts will not have been completely in vain, even if he fails to bring about a settlement.

Other personal qualities

It goes without saying that because of the nature of his work a conciliator must have the ability to get along well with people. He must, to a certain extent, be a specialist in human relations—in the relations between the parties when they come face to face, and in his own relations with them. He must be honest, polite, tactful, self-confident, even-tempered and patient in trying to accomplish results. He should have the patience to listen to what the parties say and want to say, to long and sometimes tedious and irrelevant discussions. He should obviously have powers of persuasion, including a good command of language and facility of expression, and should be able to communicate with the parties in language they understand.

A conciliator deals with the leading figures in the world of industry in his country, and has to preside over their joint meetings in conciliation proceedings. Therefore he not only needs tact and the ability to guide and control their joint discussions; he must also give an impression of experience, responsibility, clear-headedness and mature judgement. It may also be especially noted that he deals with practical men of affairs, and must be able to show them that he possesses enough plain common sense and practical-mindedness.

Certain other qualities can be cited which it would be desirable for a conciliator to have. In the informal atmosphere of conciliation a friendly personality is, for example, a distinct asset. A sense of humour can be helpful on the same account, especially for relieving the tensions of joint discussions. A special alacrity of mind will enable a conciliator to grasp quickly and analyse rapidly the main elements of controversy. But it would be totally unrealistic to say that he must possess all these qualities. What may perhaps be important is a power of critical self-analysis ; a conciliator must be able to look at himself honestly and sincerely to recognise the positive qualities of his own character and personality that he can rely upon, as well as to realise his limitations and to discover whether he can remedy his deficiencies and how to go about it.

PROFESSIONAL QUALIFICATIONS

A conciliator should also possess certain professional qualifications. In view of the nature of this work, he must see himself as a repository of knowledge and experience. If he is to discharge his responsibility to its fullest extent, the parties must look upon him with high regard for his professional competence.

Knowledge of industry and of the industrial relations system

Needless to say, a conciliator should be fully familiar with the law and regulations concerning industrial relations and the settlement of industrial disputes in his country. He should also be familiar with the practical side of his country's industrial relations system, e.g. the development and structure of trade unions and employers' associations; the prevailing methods of collective bargaining; negotiating procedures and practices; the operation of agreed negotiating bodies set up by the parties; and the main causes and patterns of disputes.

Where the prevailing system of collective bargaining includes or is largely based on negotiations at the plant level, or where the conciliation service deals with disputes arising at that level, a conciliator needs also to be familiar with the conduct of labour relations within individual undertakings. He should have some knowledge of personnel management, the functioning of trade unions within undertakings, the role of shop stewards or local trade union representatives, any other system of workers' representation, grievance and disciplinary procedures and joint consultation machinery.

It is important that his basic training should include a general background of industrial experience which enables him to understand the management process. He should have some knowledge of the products and services, the production methods, practices and nomenclature of the industries with which he is concerned. This can enable him to make an easier approach to the parties, and experience shows that it is helpful for a conciliator to be able to speak their language and not to be a complete novice to their world. It is not, of course, recommended that a conciliator should acquire a thorough knowledge of production methods and processes, and indeed any attempt on his part to do so for the purposes of his work can be a waste of time and effort.

A closely related concomitant to knowledge of an industry is knowledge of the occupations and employment practices within the industry. All too frequently disputes have as their point of origin pay for tedious occupations, unsafe and unhealthy conditions, undue muscular fatigue, and innumerable other points directly connected with job content. Questions of permanent, temporary and casual employment, occupational advancement and transfers, manning arrangements and workloads are other matters that come in for their share of workers' demands or complaints. It is quite obvious that the conciliator can make little if any contribution to a settlement if he has no knowledge of the matters under discussion.

Naturally, since most disputes concern wage rates and other financial matters, a conciliator should be familiar with economic questions and financial considerations. In certain industries questions of technological change, productivity, incentive schemes or other highly technical questions arise fairly often, and in that case a conciliator should arm himself with some background knowledge of these questions as part of his basic technical qualifications.

In societies that are in course of industrialisation some of the factors that generally influence relations between employers and workers are not normally encountered in industrially advanced countries. It is therefore important for conciliators in developing countries to have some understanding of those factors, especially traditional outlooks and cultural peculiarities, and of the way in which they affect labour relations.

Ability to profit from experience and research

A conciliator begins his career with a certain amount of professional competence, depending on his educational background, his previous training and his experience. Before being assigned to handle cases he will have been given some basic training on his new function, and the conciliation service may have a programme for further training of its staff. Although such training is important, it can only supplement the efforts that a conciliator himself will need to make to improve his professional competence, and there will naturally be a greater need for him to make such efforts if the conciliation service does not have a training programme.

In his work a conciliator will mainly have to draw on his own experience. He will be handling various types of cases and will be exposed to a wide variety of situations. In dealing with a case he can employ techniques he has found useful in previous cases. He will be continually refining those techniques, and he can also experiment with new ones. As he gains experience he will build up a fund of options or alternatives to cope with particular situations. In order to derive the utmost benefits from his experience, however, he will need to make a conscious effort to study, analyse and draw lessons from it.

Case experience is invaluable, and there are a number of labour relations observers who believe that this is the only knowledge that adds to a conciliator's innate ability. This appears to be an exaggeration, and may hold good only for exceptionally talented conciliators who have more than their share of human wisdom. Certainly a conciliator can learn from the experiences of other conciliators and from other sources of information.

A fundamental aspect of a conciliator's professional competence is his ability to form judgements. After taking up a case, and in the course of the proceedings, a conciliator has to take decisions on many questions. Broadly, he has to decide on his preparations for the case, what is to be his strategy in conducting the proceedings and how to bring about an accommodation between the parties. Within these broad fields he has to decide on matters of detail ; even his choice of a technique in a particular situation involves the exercise of discretion. The views and suggestions he wants to convey to the parties require delicate and discriminating exercise of judgement, as do the place, time and manner of communicating them. Because of the wide variety of questions and situations with which he has to deal, a conciliator's judgement also needs to be versatile.

It should be noted that disputes are not only a matter of differences between the parties. They are at bottom and fundamentally problems of human behaviour and group relations. A conciliator is concerned with problems of labour and human relations which are highly dynamic and of unusual complexity. He is concerned with companies, trade unions and employers' associations as social institutions, with problems of organisational behaviour and leadership roles. More specifically, he is concerned with the problems of the parties' attitudes—towards the dispute itself and the issues involved, towards each other and towards himself.

A conciliator can improve his ability and versatility to make judgements by a fuller understanding of these problems. It is possible that after many years' experience in his work he may acquire a kind of intuitive knowledge about them. There are, however, limitations to the knowledge that a conciliator can acquire from personal experience and observations alone. He can also refer himself to a growing body of "scientific" knowledge in the social sciences, notably economics, including labour economics, and the branches of sociology and psychology especially concerned with the problems of industry, social institutions, group behaviour and cultural change.

In recent years sociological, psychological and inter-disciplinary studies of the labour and human problems of industry have increased tremendously. An increasing number of these studies are being made in developing countries, and a conciliator should be acquainted with the results of studies in his own country. To date, however, many more of these studies have been carried out in industrially advanced countries, and it is of course questionable how far the findings are relevant to developing countries. While caution is needed to sift out findings due to conditions peculiar to the countries in which the studies were made, not infrequently there will be findings which will also be useful for developing countries.

THE CONCILIATOR'S PREPARATIONS

4

A conciliator will need to make two kinds of preparations : the general preparations not related to any particular dispute and the specific preparations for a dispute in which he is to intervene.

PRE-DISPUTE READINESS

The purpose of a conciliator's general preparations is to enable him to be ready at any time to intervene in any dispute, and to facilitate his specific preparations for it. Such pre-dispute readiness is essentially a matter of having readily at hand information that the conciliator may need when he has to intervene in a dispute, and knowing where to obtain information. General preparations are therefore mainly concerned with the keeping of files, records and documentation. When these are well kept and systematically arranged, the time spent in locating any desired information is considerably reduced.

Desirability of information services

Although in dealing with a particular dispute a conciliator works alone and independently, in practice his general preparations depend to a great extent on the organisation of the conciliation service, particularly as regards record-keeping and the provision of documentation and information for individual members of its staff.

For that purpose it is important that the conciliation service should be efficiently organised and provided with specialised staff who can at short notice assemble, analyse and provide the conciliator with the information required and undertake detailed research when necessary. Much of this work of collecting, assembling and analysing information is probably most easily accomplished when the conciliation service is within the ministry or department of labour, with the latter's statistical and research services at its disposal. This research function, which should be part of the general responsibility of the service, is also important for the formulation of industrial relations policy.

Ideally, the headquarters of the service should serve as a central documentation and information service for all conciliators at headquarters and in the field. Many of the arrangements suggested in the following pages can also be made by a regional office to which a number of conciliators are assigned. A conciliator with sole responsibility for a region and no central service to draw upon will necessarily have to make his own arrangements.

Background information required

Conciliators should be able to draw on various kinds of background information, including information on current events and developments in industries with which they are concerned.

(a) On employers and trade unions

Conciliators should be able to draw on various kinds of background information concerning employers and trade unions that may be parties to disputes coming up for conciliation.

In the case of a regional office it would be useful to maintain a card index of employing establishments in the region. The index may include in respect of each establishment information on such matters as ownership (individual, corporate, direct or indirect, private or public), type of business, products, membership of employers' associations, number of workers, the union or unions to which they belong and their affiliation, the recognised union or unions, collective bargaining situation and disputes in which the establishment has been involved.

If there are quite a number of trade unions in the area with members in more than one establishment, a card index of trade unions may also be established containing in respect of each organisation information on such matters as its affiliation, number of members (if available), establishments in which it has members, members of the executive body and principal officers, collective bargaining relations, and disputes and strikes in which the union has been involved.

(b) On agreements, awards and wage orders

A conciliator should have readily available to him copies of collective agreements concluded by direct negotiations, as well as of conciliation settlements and arbitration awards, especially those arrived at within the area or relating to the industries for which he is responsible. In countries where a system of statutory wage fixing is in operation he should have copies of minimum wage orders. If other government bodies issue decisions bearing on industrial relations, copies of those decisions should be available also. The value of all these documents lies in the fact that they provide comparative data which may be relevant to the issues in dispute. Well drafted clauses in collective agreements can serve as models for future agreements.

To facilitate the consultation of these documents it is desirable that they should be analysed and the various provisions dealing with particular items filed separately. For example, in the case of collective agreements, there could be a compilation of the clauses dealing with union security, and separate compilations dealing with wages, hours and overtime, fringe benefits (i.e. paid sick leave, paid holidays, etc.), seniority, grievance procedures and so forth.

A conciliator (or the office to which he is attached) should take note of current collective agreements within his jurisdiction and of their dates of expiry. It can be expected that negotiations for the renewal of an agreement may begin before its expiration date, and he will thus have a forewarning of the negotiations that will take place in the very near future and in which he may eventually be involved.

(c) On past negotiations and disputes between particular parties

In dealing with a dispute a conciliator has to consider its background. This includes the previous negotiations and disputes between the parties. It is normal practice to open a file for a dispute and to keep records of disputes handled by the conciliation service. When a file is opened for a dispute that is the first to occur between the parties it will be important to keep the file alive by adding to it material concerning the subsequent development of their relationship. This material will include the agreements reached by direct negotiations and records of disputes that subsequently arise between them, i.e. reports of conciliators, settlements reached by conciliation, submission of disputes to arbitration, arbitration awards, information on strikes and lockouts, etc.

Such a file becomes a sort of case history of the relationship between the parties concerned, and should be consulted each time a dispute arises between them. The objective should be to build up such a record or case history for every collective bargaining relationship between particular parties. In due course there will thus come to be case histories for the relations between all parties between whom there can occur disputes in which conciliators are likely to intervene. While the records will be important mainly for conciliation, they will also be of great use for "preventive conciliation", which will be discussed in a later chapter.

(d) On current developments and trends

A conciliator has to keep abreast of developments that are likely to affect the relations between employers and workers or to have a bearing on collective bargaining demands and industrial disputes.

The local offices of the labour inspection service are most important sources of information on developments affecting the labour situation in their respective areas. Labour inspectors are in a position to learn from their visits whether in any undertaking labour trouble is brewing that should be quickly brought to the notice of the conciliation service. The immediate relaying of such information to the conciliation service must be provided for.

Certain important developments may be reported in newspapers and periodicals of general circulation, but the conciliator has to look primarily to special publications for the kind of information he needs. The list that follows is not all-inclusive and may include sources not available in all countries.

● Publications of trade unions, management and employers' associations, including annual reports and proceedings of meetings of such organisations.

These are relatively good indicators of trends. The attitudes of the sponsoring groups are frequently reflected in the tone of the articles and editorials.

Trade union organs are very useful sources of information on new developments regarding the organisation concerned (decisions taken by the executive, changes in union leadership or policy, formation of a splinter group, etc.) and often on the trade union movement at large.

● Publications of professional and technical societies, i.e. industrial relations societies, industrial relations research associations, and institutes or associations of personnel management.

These are technical publications and are useful to the conciliator in his efforts to increase his technical competence. They also often contain information on or articles analysing important current problems, developments and trends.

● Research monographs on industrial relations subjects issued by government bureaux, university faculties and private institutions and foundations.

These can be invaluable sources of information concerning specific aspects of industrial relations. There are still only a few developing countries where significant advances in industrial relations research have been made, but interest in it is growing in many parts of the world. A paper or monograph that will be of direct relevance to a pending case may be rare, but an alert conciliator can gain valuable information for later use from a work that may appear to be of little immediate interest.

- Wage and salary surveys, especially those carried out for wage boards or committees or conducted on a regular periodic basis to provide current information.

For a conciliator these surveys at least provide points of reference. This may sound as if their value to him may not be of much consequence. However, in trying to influence the attitude of either party, a conciliator will need some reference point for leverage ; and there will always be occasions when a creative conciliator can use any bit of information for that purpose.

- Legislative enactments, administrative regulations, decisions of administrative bodies.
- Proceedings of conferences, symposia, seminars, etc., dealing with industrial relations subjects.

SPECIFIC CASE PREPARATION

The effectiveness of a conciliator in his handling of a case depends to a very great extent on the way he prepares himself for it. Case preparation involves taking all possible steps to be ready to cope with whatever may occur in the conduct of the conciliation proceedings. It should be realised that no two disputes are ever alike in every material respect. There can be important similarities between the dispute in which a conciliator is involved at any given time and one he has handled before, and experience in the previous dispute may be useful for the current one ; but he should guard against being misled by the similarities. He may think that because substantially similar issues are involved he can afford to be lax in making his preparations for the current dispute. This would clearly be dangerous if the parties to the two disputes are different, but it would be no less dangerous if they are the same ; in the latter case even if the issues appear similar, there will invariably be differences in certain circumstances. The most prudent course for a conciliator to follow is to start from the premise that each dispute is unique, and to make the most complete preparations for it.

Part of the work of case preparation is done on the basis of available office files and records. It is continued in the initial or preliminary contacts with the parties, and may involve seeking out further information by other means where necessary. It should be emphasised that all this preparatory work can be started when it is known that negotiations are taking place between the parties and when the dispute is still at an incipient stage, or before it comes into the open.

Case folder

Almost the first concrete step of a conciliator when taking up a case is the preparation of the case folder which he brings with him to his meetings with the parties. There is normally no particular difficulty in preparing this although in his first cases the conciliator will have to give particular attention to it. It will contain his basic working papers : copies of the documents which may have been received from either or both of the parties (the report of the dispute, the strike or lockout notice, the request for assistance, the trade union demands or proposals, etc.) ; material or his notes containing the information which he should have readily at hand, and his notes on the progress of the proceedings and particularly the important points brought out in the discussions.

Information to be collected

The conciliator must provide himself with as full information as possible about the dispute, its background, the parties, the facts and the issues involved. One essential point must be emphasised : he must not on the basis of this information prejudge the issues or the merits of the controversy.

(a) On the background and facts of the dispute

The conciliator will need to know as much as possible about the background and facts of the dispute. A dispute appears as a difference between the parties over the issue or issues involved, but it may have underlying causes, often sociological or psychological, which are not clearly apparent. It may be merely a symptom of a more deep-seated disorder in the parties' relationship or a culmination of accumulated workers' grievances and frustrations. Where the relations between the management and the workers have not been very good, even a minor or trifling incident may be sufficient to spark off a major conflict. A conciliator should therefore guard against being deceived by the superficial appearance of a dispute, and should not regard it as being merely a difference over the issue or issues specified by the parties. He should try to find out whether there are underlying causes and should seek to understand them, for they can substantially affect the manner in which he can bring about a settlement.

Some of the information which the conciliator needs may have been given by the parties in reporting the dispute or when requesting assistance. For the background, he will consult existing office files and records concerning the parties, or the case history of their relationship referred to earlier. He will have kept himself informed of any previous negotiations between the parties concerning the dispute of which he has become aware. Otherwise he will have to find out whether and how such negotiations have taken place. He will also ascertain whether there is any likelihood of a work stoppage.

If the dispute concerns an industry into which the conciliator is being thrust for the first time, he should make at least a partial study of it and acquire some familiarity with its products, operations and economic position. The conciliator can gain a better understanding of the entire industry if he is acquainted with the operations and processes that precede and follow those carried on in the branch of the industry with which he is directly concerned. This knowledge will give him some indication of the repercussions of a possible stoppage; if the industry performs one of a series of closely related operations or processes, a strike is all the more likely to have regional or national repercusions. Also, if the dispute relates to an occupation or an aspect of conditions of employment with which he has no previous familiarity, he will have to make a partial study of it and obtain as much information as possible about it.

(b) On the issues

The conciliator will also consult the available office records for information and comparative data that have a bearing on the issues involved in the dispute the relevant provisions of collective agreements, conciliation settlements, awards, court decisions, wage orders or legislation; data and statistics on wages paid in other establishments in the same industry, and in other industries in the area where the dispute occurs, in the case of wage issues; similar comparative data on any industrial practices in other industries, when the issues relate to such practices. The extent to which he will need to obtain further information from other sources is a matter of judgement for the conciliator, and depends on the adequacy of the information already available from the office records. The question of how much detail or information he will note down for his case folder is also a matter of judgement.

(c) On personalities

It is important for a conciliator to have some idea of the kind of persons he will be dealing with in the dispute, the extent of their experience of negotiations and the conditions affecting their roles as leaders in their organisations. He will therefore seek this information with regard to any of the parties whom he does not know. It may well be that it is the first time he is handling a case involving certain persons; if so, other conciliators who have previously worked with them are naturally excellent sources of information; the files on past negotiations can also be most useful, as are also contacts with other management and trade union leaders.

THE CONCILIATOR'S ENTRY INTO A DISPUTE

5

The active intervention of a conciliator in a dispute takes the form of holding conciliation meetings for substantive discussion of the issues. There are, however, certain preliminary steps to be completed before a conciliator begins : a decision has to be taken to submit a dispute to conciliation, a conciliator has to be assigned to the case, and he must make his preparations for it, very often including the establishment of initial or exploratory contacts with the parties. The present chapter is concerned with some of these preliminary steps.

INITIATION OF CONCILIATION PROCEEDINGS

In general, the conciliation procedure may be set in motion on the initiative of any of the parties to the dispute, or ex officio by the conciliation authority. In various countries the law requires reports of disputes or advance notice of proposed strikes or lockouts to be given to the conciliation authority. Such reports or notices may provide the basis for intervention ; but even where they have not been given, the conciliation authority is generally empowered to take cognisance of the disputes that arise.

Timing

The timing of intervention is normally no problem, except if no request has been received from the parties and if conciliation is not prescribed by law. Where a government conciliation service nevertheless exists, it must then decide whether assistance should be offered ; and that is a matter of judgement.

If the dispute is one that affects or threatens to affect some vital public service, the conciliation service may have little alternative to intervention. In certain circumstances, however, it is important to avoid intervening prematurely. In certain countries the government encourages the parties to establish agreed procedures for the prevention and settlement of disputes through collective bargaining. Where such an agreed procedure exists, it should be followed and exhausted before a dispute is reported to the government conciliation service. Any attempt by one of the parties to by-pass the procedure will undermine its authority and eventually lead to its falling into disuse. A conciliation service should therefore resist any attempt to make it intervene prematurely. A conciliator should, however, be available to assist the parties when there has been a breakdown of the procedure, not by going into the merits of the dispute but by proposing ways and means of reverting to the procedure that is established.

Even in cases where there is no agreed procedure for settling disputes, the parties should be encouraged to achieve a settlement by themselves. This suggestion is based on the general conception that it is preferable for the parties to reach agreement by their own efforts and to have resort to outside assistance only when they have failed to do so. This is particularly true where the parties have already had some experience of collective bargaining, and when it may be expected that their negotiations can lead to some concrete results without the aid of a third party.

The timing of intervention may be affected by strikes and lockouts. It is a great temptation to conciliators, when a serious stoppage of work has actually started, to rush into the arena and endeavour to bring about immediate peace. Paradoxical though it may seem, however, immediate intervention may be entirely appropriate when a strike is not imminent but not effective when one has just begun. It is impossible to lay down rigid rules in this respect because so much depends on the circumstances of the case ; and the decision is one which can be taken only in the light of those circumstances, and of experience and knowledge of the parties involved.

To give one example, a strike may have started after lengthy negotiations have broken down, and the parties may be in such a bitter or stubborn frame of mind that they are determined to stand by their respective positions. In that event it is unlikely that for the first few days they will be in a mood to consider any compromise solution, and they may therefore be quite impervious to any arguments which may be put forward by an outsider. Furthermore, acceptance of conciliation at that stage may be regarded as a sign of weakness, and a stoppage may have to go on for some little time until both parties begin to feel its impact and realise that no progress is being made ; at that point attitudes will probably begin to change and conciliation may be started with a reasonable prospect of serious discussions between the parties.

On the other hand, it is also possible to be unduly reticent about offering a conciliator's services once collective bargaining has failed. Even if neither party takes the initiative, it should be possible by discreet enquiries to find out whether the parties do not really want conciliation. Not infrequently both parties do, but each is afraid that it would be interpreted as a sign of weakness to make the first move. One side or the other may thus be ready to tell the conciliator in confidence that it would welcome an initiative from him. This is a form of face-saving, thanks to which a conciliator can play an effective role in starting on the road to settlement a dispute that might have remained in a state of deadlock indefinitely.

In a number of countries where disputes have to be reported to the conciliation authority the reports are required to contain certain details, partly to enable the conciliation authority to decide whether there exists an "industrial dispute", as defined by law, for which conciliation can be made available. If a report which shows that a dispute clearly exists does not contain all the details required, it is of course possible to refer the report back to the party submitting it and to request the missing details. However, this can mean unnecessary delay ; it also smacks of bureaucracy, of which the conciliation process should be entirely free. It would seem better to have the dispute assigned immediately to a conciliator, who can thus begin his preparations for it and proceed to have initial contacts with the parties, through which he can obtain whatever necessary information has not been given in the report.

Assignment of cases

The practice in some countries is to assign conciliators to particular industries or groups of industries, so that they acquire intimate knowledge of conditions in the industries assigned to them. Under another arrangement the country is divided into regions, and a conciliator is assigned to a region and made responsible for disputes arising in his territorial jurisdiction. Under both of these systems the conciliator concerned may enter a case under his own authority, either on the basis of a request from a party to the dispute or on his own initiative. In other cases conciliators receive their assignment from a superior officer, who takes the decision about intervening in any dispute. This method is usually followed by the headquarters of the conciliation service and by any regional office whose staff includes a number of conciliators.

In these cases, information about disputes will normally be considered in the first instance by the superior officer, who will in the light of current circumstances decide who among his staff should undertake a particular assignment. Among the factors to be taken into consideration are the availability of individual conciliators, e.g. the extent to which they are already involved in current disputes, and any particular specialised knowledge or experience which they may have and which may seem relevant to the dispute in question. However, even where provision has been made for regional conciliation offices or regional conciliators, it is often the practice to assign senior or more experienced conciliators from the headquarters staff to deal with major disputes occurring in any part of the country. In countries where the conciliation service has been set up to specialise in conciliation and related functions the head of the service is often himself an active conciliator personally taking charge of disputes of major importance.

In some instances the parties may approach directly, or express a preference for, a conciliator with whom they have already had dealings in the past. Because he obviously has been able to win their trust and confidence, their wishes should be respected unless there are strong reasons for not doing so.

PRELIMINARY CONTACTS WITH THE PARTIES

Once he has been assigned to a case, the conciliator will usually need to make preliminary contact with the parties separately. The purpose of this preliminary contact is threefold : to give them information, to obtain information from them, and to establish his relationship with them on a positive note. It is on the basis of these preliminary contacts with the parties, together with the information he has obtained from office files and records and other sources, that the conciliator prepares his next moves and tentatively decides how he shall act.

The conciliator must make careful preparations for these contacts, which should normally be made in every case unless for exceptional reasons he has to hold conciliation meetings immediately. He has to decide whether he should meet the parties personally or merely speak to them over the telephone. Face-to-face meetings will be essential where he needs to establish a personal relationship with the parties or when he has a special message to give to each of them, as in a case in which they are involved in a dispute or in conciliation proceedings for the first time, where he is dealing with them for the first time as parties to a dispute, or where fairly complicated issues are involved and exploratory discussions cannot be adequately carried out by telephone.

A normal procedure would be for the conciliator to telephone to the leading representatives of both parties and ask them to meet him separately for informal discussions in his office. In inviting them to meet him, he might explain that the discussions would be merely exploratory and not part of the normal conciliation procedure, in which the parties would be fully represented by their negotiating committees. He might therefore suggest that the number of representatives at this stage should be kept as small as possible—preferably not more than two or three from each side. It must, however, be accepted that this is a matter for the parties to decide, and if they wish to bring more than the number suggested by him the conciliator should not insist, since such insistence might create the wrong atmosphere.

Alternatively, it would also be perfectly normal for the conciliator to call on the parties at their offices. In many cases this may be more convenient for them, and enable them to save time. It is also possible that only one of the parties can send representatives to the conciliator's office, and that the conciliator has to call on the representatives of the other party at their office. No hard and fast rules can be suggested as to the way in which the conciliator should make his first approach ; he will take into account such other considerations as his past relationship with the parties or degree of familiarity with them, the proximity of his office to the parties' offices, their anticipated reaction to his entry into the case, the availability of their spokesmen and his case load.

As indicated earlier, the initial, exploratory contacts provide the conciliator with an opportunity to give information to the parties, to obtain information from them and to establish good working relations with them. It must be emphasised that these purposes are served together throughout his discussions with them, by the questions he puts to them and by his observation of their behaviour ; in giving or obtaining information he is also establishing his relationship with the parties. Nevertheless, it is useful, for emphasis and clarity, to consider these purposes separately.

Giving information

The conciliator informs the parties of his entry into the case and of the fact that his services are available to help them towards a settlement. It is appropriate that he should emphasise the impartial nature of his role and his objective of helping them to arrive at an agreed settlement. The information he will give to the parties will naturally depend on the extent of their experience of negotiations or conciliation. If they are experienced negotiators, he will not need to give them a long explanation about his role and the procedure of conciliation. However, he may find an opening to suggest that further direct talks without his assistance may produce good results, and he may indicate the lines which such further negotiations might follow. This possibility can arise when the parties have been so immersed in detailed argument over one or two issues that they miss a point which holds the possibility of a solution and which becomes apparent to a detached observer reviewing the course of the previous negotiations.

The conciliator faces a different situation when the parties have had no substantial previous experience of collective relations, and the situation is particularly delicate if it is the first time they are involved in an industrial dispute or in conciliation proceedings. Either or both of the parties may not even know of the existence of the government conciliation service, or may have no idea at all of the conciliation process and how they should participate in it. The conciliator may therefore need to explain government policy for the settlement of disputes, what conciliation is all about, how the parties participate in it and what is to be his role. More particularly, he should explain how he will proceed, how the parties will be represented and what may be expected during joint meetings, especially as regards the parties' behaviour toward each other. He may, for example, advise that vehement or even intemperate language may be expected but that such things are not exceptional and that the parties should not allow themselves to become unduly excited. He should encourage them to ask him questions to clarify any point on which they may be in doubt, since his object is to help them prepare to take part in the proceedings in the most productive way possible.

At times, one or both of the parties will want to obtain from the conciliator his opinion of the other party and of the issues in the case. No clear, definable line can be easily drawn regarding the extent to which the conciliator should answer such questions. However, he may find it useful to bear in mind that his personal views on a particular subject can be more or less concealed by generalisations.

Obtaining information

Through his initial contacts the conciliator can acquire from each of the parties as much further information as possible about the background and facts of the dispute, including the attempts the parties may have made to settle it between them, their understanding of the issues involved, and the parties themselves. In the absence of office records concerning any previous negotiations and disputes between the parties, he should also seek to obtain information on the past history of their relations.

Another important objective of the conciliator in the initial contacts is to explore the parties' attitudes as regards the dispute and the issues, and towards each other. He obtains information concerning the parties' attitudes not only from what they say but also from their conduct—their tones of voice, their facial expressions, their gestures. The practised eye and ear of an alert, observant conciliator will find much to note. In many countries it is not unusual for a union to include certain items in its demands simply as trading points or as "throw-away" items. Similarly, a company's counter-proposals may include items for bargaining purposes only, on which it does not intend to take a serious stand. A conciliator will have to find out as early as possible the parties' real attitudes on the issues ; otherwise he may be misled in his search for areas of agreement.

It is also important for the conciliator to know what the parties feel about his role. It makes a lot of difference whether they welcome his intervention or whether either or both are hostile to his stepping into their dispute. The lot of a conciliator is often a hard one, and he must be prepared for occasions when the parties regard him as an unwanted intruder. Having become aware of the adverse attitude of either or both of the parties, he can adjust his approach to overcome this particular difficulty. It will, of course, be necessary in the first place for him to find out the cause of such an adverse attitude ; that will have to be done diplomatically.

In trying to induce either of the parties to provide information, the conciliator should avoid putting into his questions any overtones of harassment or inquisition. Too frequently an inexperienced conciliator, on encountering a hostile or decidedly cool reception to his entry, reacts in an aggressive manner and becomes demanding in his inquiries. The conciliator must learn to make inquiries in a conversational matter-of-fact way that does not smack of a law officer's investigation and cross-examination. If a question on a matter of importance goes unheeded, he can always come back to it, phrasing his question in different language. One of the main advantages of his using this method is that the principal roles in conciliation proceedings then manifestly devolve on the parties. It may also provide the opening which the conciliator is seeking.

The conciliator may consider it important to have a record of the information he has obtained ; but on the assumption that the information has been given in confidence, he should be very discreet in taking notes. Moreover, note-taking in the course of a conversation can discourage spontaneity on the part of the person whom he is meeting. The conciliator should limit his note-taking to the barest minimum, and it should in any case be done in a very casual manner. There are people who have a talent for mentally cataloguing the highlights of a discussion which they put down in writing later on. A conciliator should try to develop this ability.

Establishing working relations

It must again be emphasised that the conciliator's relationship with the parties is essentially a matter of trust and confidence. The initial contacts serve in establishing the conciliator's acceptability to the parties ; they provide him with an opportunity to start his relationship with them on a wholesome, positive note. His aim must be to give the parties a good impression of him and of his professional competence and his integrity and impartiality.

The conciliator should not allow his appearance to lose him the parties' respect for him as a person, since that would inevitably affect their attitude towards him as a conciliator. He must therefore adjust his personal appearance to the image he needs to project, depending on local conditions and customs. It is largely a question of grooming (including personal hygiene) and of dress.

The tone of the conciliator's relationship with the parties can be set by his approach. That is why it is important that in these initial contacts it should be impressed on the parties that the conciliator relies on their voluntary co-operation. Regardless of the nature of the information he seeks to obtain from them, he should never assume the role of an investigator or enforcement officer. At the slightest hint of coercion, even unwilling or accidental, the parties may adopt a hostile attitude towards him, and the opportunity for effective conciliation will have been seriously jeopardised.

In order to establish working relations with the parties, the conciliator needs to bear in mind at least two points. In the first place he must show a sympathetic concern with the dispute as a problem for the parties. The case may be only one of several disputes with which he is currently concerned, but he must realise that for the parties it is likely to be a major problem. If he gives the appearance of regarding the dispute as a routine matter, his attitude will hardly stimulate their interest in his intervention and in discussing the issues with him. They must feel that he is fully interested in hearing their version of what has taken place up to that point. Otherwise his manner must be polite and businesslike, yet not aloof but personal and friendly.

Secondly, there is a need to demonstrate that the conciliator understands the issues. During the initial contacts, he will be offered opportunities to display some knowledge of the problems involved. This is a very subtle opening for the conciliator; it underscores a point made earlier about acquiring a broad background of industrial experience. If the conciliator is regarded as knowledgeable, within the framework of his assignment, it is more likely that the parties will welcome his intervention. Statements by the conciliator that are brief and to the point have a much better chance of drawing a favourable reaction than monologues that seem designed to be show-pieces to impress listeners.

Finally, a properly timed ending to a meeting, a visit or a telephone conversation can leave a positive impression. When the conciliator is satisfied that he has provided the parties with all the information he has planned to give them and that they understand what assistance he may provide, when he also has received all the information he believes possible to obtain at that stage, and when he has provided a basis for holding conciliation meetings with them, the encounter should be closed.

TYPES OF MEETINGS AND ARRANGEMENTS FOR THEM

6

In pursuing his objective of promoting the settlement of a dispute, the conciliator performs a number of procedural functions relating to the scheduling, arranging and conduct of meetings with the parties.[1] In this chapter we shall consider the types of meetings a conciliator may organise and the arrangements and preparations to be made for meetings, while the conduct of meetings will be dealt with in the next chapter.

TYPES OF MEETINGS

There are normally two types of meeting which a conciliator may hold with the parties to a dispute : joint conferences attended by both parties and separate meetings with only one party. In certain circumstances he may resort to meetings of a third type—private meetings with the minimum number of participants. Each type of meeting possesses certain characteristics and relative advantages and disadvantages.

Joint conferences

The joint conference, at which the conciliator acts as chairman, is the stage of the conciliation proceedings at which the parties discuss their differences with each other. It is marked by the alignment of the parties' representatives on the opposite sides of the conference table. A joint conference is usually attended by the full membership of the two negotiating committees.

The fact that all of each party's representatives are present, the alignment of the negotiating committees on opposite sides of the table and the presence of

---

[1] William F. Simkin : *Mediation and the dynamics of collective bargaining* (Washington, Bureau of National Affairs, Inc., 1971), pp. 77-94.

the conciliator in the formal capacity of chairman—all these factors contribute to an air of formality, with its attendant features. In this situation, and especially if the negotiating committees are large, it is generally desirable that each side communicate with the other side and with the conciliator (as chairman) through a single spokesman. The conciliator will have suggested this arrangement to the parties during his initial contacts with them, and should have obtained information about the identity of the parties' spokesmen before the beginning of the first joint conference. However, he may be spared the trouble of himself arranging for the designation of spokesmen when the parties are represented by experienced negotiators.

The chief characteristic of joint conferences is the fact that the parties are usually very conscious of their positions as adversaries. At this type of meeting the parties play their antagonistic roles much more determinedly and purposefully than in separate meetings.

Each party will usually state its position on an issue in a defensive manner while making an intense assault on the opposing view. Words are carefully measured, in terms of offence and defence, and pointedly delivered.

The members of each negotiating committee will strive to maintain an appearance of solid and unflinching unity. By nods of the head or other expressive gestures or short remarks, members will show firm backing for the committee spokesman.

A joint conference will usually have its fill of dramatic moments. The exchanges between the parties will at times be marked by heated arguments. Not infrequently there will be mutual recriminations, and accusations may be defiantly hurled or dreadful hidden motives hinted at.

The joint conference provides an outlet for aggressive feelings on the part of either party. In many instances there may be no suitable way of easing hostility except direct confrontation between the parties. However, if a feeling of hostility is allowed to linger there is a risk that it may cause irreparable damage to the negotiations or to future relationships. The same danger may arise if the two sides are allowed to engage in bitter or harsh exchanges ; but such exchanges may also purge them of their hostility. This is one of the most difficult problems the conciliator has to deal with as chairman of a joint conference and in scheduling meetings.

The joint conference also provides an opportunity for the conciliator to observe the participants in their direct relationships with each other. Is there a clash of personalities between any members of the negotiating committees on the two sides? Are harsh comments from one side directed to anyone in particular on the other side? Do certain members of a committee tend to provoke from the other side less angry responses than the other members? Are some issues only mildly emphasised while others occupy more attention? Does there seem to be more emotion aroused when the other side discusses certain issues? Do the members of a negotiating committee all react in the same way to their leader or chief spokesman?

These are only a few examples of the use by the conciliator of his powers of observation with regard to the parties' behaviour at the joint conference, which can give him important clues about their attitudes to which he has to adjust his approach. If, for example, there is a clash of personalities between leading members of the negotiating committees, the conciliator may have to find out whether it has been the underlying cause of the dispute, or whether it has aggravated it.

One of the main purposes of a joint conference is to set out the unresolved issues that separate the parties. This alone may be ample reason for the conciliator to schedule such a meeting. When the conciliator takes up the case, the unsolved issues will be those remaining after the parties' preceding bilateral negotiations. These issues will be spelled out at the first joint conference. When the issues are numerous or particularly complex, there is no substitute for a joint conference to obtain a clear statement of the issues that remain to be resolved.

The pace of the discussions in such a conference tends to be very slow, and where relatively complicated issues are involved there may be prolonged discussions before any real progress is made. While it may not be possible, however, to avoid prolonged discussions, there is a real advantage for the conciliator in allowing each party to view the obstinacy of the other, to feel the physical weariness of constantly re-stating their own views and of repeatedly hearing the other side's statement of inflexible opposition.

Separate meetings

A separate meeting between the conciliator and one party can arise in three ways. The most common occurrence is for such a meeting to take place in connection with a joint conference. As a general rule the initiative for holding a separate meeting is taken by the conciliator himself. At some stage of the joint meeting, the conciliator may find it useful to suspend the debate between the two parties and to meet them separately. He will then call a recess or adjourn the joint meeting, and will meet them in separate rooms, one after the other ; but separate meetings may also be arranged, for example at the request of the parties, after closed meetings[1] of each of the negotiating committees.

---

[1] Closed meetings are attended only by the members of one of the negotiating committees.

Of the other two forms of separate meeting, one occurs when the conciliator has meetings with the parties at different times, but not in connection with a joint conference. The other occurs when the two parties refuse to come together in a joint meeting but are willing to be present at the same time in the same building, though in separate rooms, as part of a process of continuous negotiation through the conciliator, who goes from room to room. This form of separate meeting is thus rather like a separate meeting held in connection with a joint conference, except that there is no joint meeting at all. This procedure was followed by the United Nations mediator on the Palestine question in 1948-49, and has come to be known in international mediation as the Rhodes formula ; in the following pages meetings of this kind will be simply referred to as meetings of the Rhodes formula type.

At a separate meeting the conciliator does not act as chairman ; he has a personal dialogue with the party present. The atmosphere is relatively free from the tensions of a joint meeting ; it is more relaxed and informal. The party present does not address its words to an opponent on the opposite side, as in a joint meeting. It does not exhibit the same combative attitude as it tends to assume in the presence of an adversary.

The separate meeting provides the conciliator with opportunities that are not present in a joint conference. He uses the separate meeting to analyse and interpret the position of the other side. To the party present he can express views and offer suggestions and advice which he could not, or only at the risk of arousing resentment on the part of one or the other party, at a joint meeting. It is at separate meetings that the parties may be willing to give him, in confidence, information which will advance the negotiations but which they will not divulge in each other's presence.

Another advantage of a separate meeting is that it gives the conciliator an opportunity to become better acquainted with the people he is dealing with, and to obtain a more or less intimate view of each negotiating committee as a group. Although a committee may have its principal spokesman, he will not necessarily be its most influential member ; the discussions within the committee may reveal the member or members whose views count more than do those of the others.

When he tries to bring about a change in the attitudes of the committees, it is important for the conciliator to know who are their more influential members.

It is essential to bear in mind that the relationship between the conciliator and either party during a separate meeting must be highly confidential : the absence of confidentiality at this stage of conciliation can nullify the effectiveness of the role of the conciliator. The parties will give the conciliator information in confidence only when they are convinced that their trust in him is not misplaced ; he must earn the parties' trust in him by his personal showing. No statute can create this feeling.

There are also disadvantages to the separate meeting. Perhaps foremost among these is the absent party's suspicion of what is taking place without its knowledge. The slightest act or word of the conciliator after a meeting with one party is carefully screened by the other party to detect any sign of siding with the former ; particular care must therefore be taken by the conciliator at that stage to protect and maintain his impartiality.

Another possible disadvantage of the separate meeting is that if there is internal conflict in a negotiating committee it may flare up at the meeting and hold up the discussion of the subjects that are at issue between the parties to the industrial dispute. The members of each negotiating committee will seek to maintain an image of complete unity when the two committees are face to face ; they will try to maintain the same appearance of unity in a separate meeting with the conciliator, but there will be occasions when differences or rivalry within the group will rise to the surface. Although it is useful for him to know of those rivalries, the conciliator must try to direct the members' attention to the main purpose of the meeting.

Private meetings

A private meeting in this context is one attended by the minimum number of the parties' representatives, preferably one from any one party. It can take the form of a joint meeting, with representatives of both sides, or of a separate meeting, with only one party represented. If the conciliator desires a private meeting he proposes it to the leading spokesman of the party concerned ; a proposal for a joint meeting should have the prior agreement of the spokesmen of both parties.

A call by the conciliator for a private meeting must be given his most careful consideration. It can serve a definite purpose, but it is no substitute for a joint conference or separate meeting. A private meeting is an exceptional measure that can be resorted to only in certain circumstances ; it should not be regarded as an additional device that is available to the conciliator in every case. If the special aura of private meetings is to be preserved, the number of such meetings that are held in a single case should be very limited.

Among the circumstances that may lead a conciliator to consider the advisability of proposing a private meeting, the following may be mentioned :

● Both in joint conferences and in separate meetings the parties have repeatedly demonstrated that they will not change their stand.

● There is a need for the conciliator to speak candidly to the leading spokesmen of the two sides, in each other's presence, regarding his observations and suggestions.

- There has been a veiled hint from either or both of the parties that a change in their thinking is possible, and that they are looking for an opportunity of obtaining advance knowledge of the other side's probable reaction.
- Even without such a hint, there is a possibility that the leader of one party might modify his declarations if he had reasonable assurance that there would be a reciprocal change on the other side.
- A point is reached where both parties must be made aware that there is no further scope for negotiation along the lines hitherto followed.

The existence of one or more of the above circumstances is not of itself sufficient reason for the conciliator to approach the parties with a suggestion for a private meeting. In addition, he must be certain of the attitude of the leaders with whom he proposes to hold the meeting, and of their control of and influence over their negotiating committees and the rank and file of their members. Thus there are really two factors that the conciliator must be capable of sensing and sizing up : the moral authority of the leaders over the negotiating committees and the remainder of the membership of the organisations involved in the dispute, and the ability of the leaders to view negotiations in the cold light of reality.

If the conciliator concludes that a private meeting will give rise only to a repetition of declarations made at previous joint conferences and separate meetings, he should not call for it. Unless there is a clear understanding on the part of all that the meeting calls for complete candour, nothing will be gained. Officially, neither of the participants will be changing its position, and there will be no promise that concessions will be forthcoming. It is understandable that the participants should not completely shed their role of advocates even in a private conversation. None the less, a clear statement of the purpose of the meeting by the conciliator will keep sparring by the parties to a minimum.

In addition, both sides should understand that the meeting best serves the interests of all concerned when only the minimum number of people know of its existence. Each person present should also be bound by the rule of honour that no reference shall ever be made to any word spoken at the meeting. Those not present at a private meeting and learning about it at some later time will have a strong tendency to think that it has resulted in major harm to their cause, and they will seldom attribute any gains to such a meeting.

The conciliator designs his role at the meeting to meet the needs of the case. There will be occasions when he alone has the information and imagination required to enable the parties to conduct a fruitful discussion. There will also be times when his major contribution will have been made by arranging the meeting, and he can play a more passive role : it is possible to foresee situations like this when the parties' concern over the problems resulting from the dispute will carry them forward. However, the conciliator must always be ready to make a major contribution.

Choice and sequence

In the course of a single case a conciliator may use any one or more of the kinds of meeting described above. Depending on the circumstances of the case and the nature of the issues involved, he may make greater use of one type of meeting than of the others. The considerations that are involved in deciding upon a meeting include what the conciliator hopes to accomplish during the meeting, the attitude of the parties as well as their convenience and availability, the time available for concluding the conciliation proceedings[1] or until a deadline is reached[2], the fact that a work stoppage has occurred, the other pressures that may affect decisions by the two sides, the conciliator's familiarity with the case, and the events that have preceded his taking up the case.

On the basis of the information he has obtained in his preparations for the case and from his initial contacts with the parties the conciliator can decide on the type of meeting he will hold first. In general, it is useful to begin with a joint conference, but there will be cases when the conciliator will find it preferable to begin with separate meetings : the nature of the issues and the circumstances may be such that he can make better progress by meeting the parties separately, bringing them together in a joint conference at a later stage. Even when the conciliator may be in favour of a joint meeting, there may be no possibility of holding it soon enough, and he may therefore have to consider the alternative of meeting the parties separately in order to get things moving without delay.

In short, a conciliator should call a meeting with clear objectives in mind. This statement refers not to his general task of resolving a dispute ; that is his ultimate objective in every assignment he undertakes. However, there are sub-objectives[3], contributing to the ultimate objective, which must be arrived at as conciliation proceeds. Meetings called by the conciliator are intended

---

[1] In cases in which time limits for concluding conciliation proceedings are laid down in laws or regulations.

[2] In the event of the expiration of an existing collective agreement or of the period set in a strike or lockout notice.

[3] Discussed more fully in Chapter 8.

to assist him in working towards these objectives. They can serve this purpose when the conciliator selects the type of meeting that meets the needs of the moment. The benefit derived from meetings can be immeasurably increased if the conciliator bears in mind the characteristics and advantages, as well as the pitfalls, of the various types among which he can choose.

ARRANGEMENTS AND PREPARATIONS

Place of meeting

Joint conferences should normally be held on premises that can be regarded as neutral ground. This can best be ensured by arranging for them to take place at the offices of the conciliation service, and that should be the normal practice. This is particularly important in countries where concilation procedures have been only relatively recently established and where it is essential to take every precaution not only to ensure that the proceedings are being conducted in a fair and impartial manner but to make it clear to all concerned that they are not improperly influenced by either party.

In cases involving experienced negotiators, however, there can be rather more flexibility in this respect. Sometimes it may be convenient to hold joint meetings on the premises of an employer, or of an employers' association or a trade union, or occasionally at a hotel.

If the parties to the dispute agree among themselves on some meeting place, freely and without any suggestion of duress, the conciliator should not object ; in such circumstances the parties, despite the fact that they may be in dispute, generally have a good mutual understanding and will not be influenced in their attitudes by the choice of premises.

As a general rule, separate meetings with the parties at different times should be held in the conciliator's office or on the premises of the conciliation service. Having regard to the convenience of the parties and his own work schedule, the conciliator should also be prepared in appropriate circumstances to meet the parties at their respective offices. As in the case of a joint conference, separate meetings of the Rhodes formula type should be held on neutral ground.

Accommodation

In a joint conference it is always possible that the two negotiating committees may want to separate so that the members of each committee can consult among themselves in closed meetings, or that the conciliator may wish to hold separate meetings with the two sides. Ideally, therefore, the accommodation for a joint conference should include three rooms—one for the joint meeting itself and the other two for the parties, closed meetings and separate meetings with the conciliator. Where this is not possible there should be a minimum of two rooms—one for the joint meeting, to serve also as one party's meeting room, and the second as the meeting room for the other party.

The joint conference room should be sufficiently large to accommodate the two negotiating committees in comfort. The rooms for the parties' closed or separate meetings should be near enough to be easily accessible, but should not be actually adjoining, since discussions in one room must not be overheard by people in the other.

Invitations to meetings

The normal ways of inviting the parties to meetings are by telephone, where that means of communication is available, and by letter. The telephone is undoubtedly preferable because it is faster, and meeting times convenient to both parties are more easily arranged by that means. It would be useful to confirm arrangements in writing. Written communications should not be stiffly formal, and the use of peremptory language should be avoided ; there should not be any hint or suggestion that the parties are being ordered to attend.

In certain countries the conciliator is in fact empowered to compel the parties to attend conciliation proceedings. Even in that case, it is advisable that the conciliator should normally follow the more informal procedure suggested above. In general, parties are willing to participate in conciliation proceedings voluntarily, and any element of compulsion can only arouse a negative attitude on their part. If used at all, compulsory powers should be reserved for exceptional cases, and after it has become clearly evident that the party concerned is simply disregarding the conciliation authority.

Number and powers of representatives

As a general rule, the smaller the number of persons present at a conciliation meeting the greater are the chances of orderly discussion and effective negotiations. The conciliator may therefore suggest to the parties, preferably during his initial contacts with them, what number of representatives it would be desirable to have at the conciliation meetings. The number will vary according to the circumstances of each case, but ideally each party's negotiating committee should not exceed four or five members. In interest disputes the parties will usually be represented by the negotiating committees that took part in the previous negotiations. In making this suggestion the conciliator should make it clear that it is none the less for each party to decide on the number of its representatives, and he should accept the parties' decisions in this respect with a good grace.

It is also desirable that the parties' representatives attending concilation meetings should possess full authority from the employers and workers concerned to reach a settlement on their behalf. In the course of his initial contacts with the parties the conciliator may suggest that such full authority is desirable. There will, however, be cases in which the authority of the representatives is limited to the conclusion of a provisional agreement subject to ratification by the side concerned. The existence of this reservation on either or both sides should be made clear at the beginning of the conciliation proceedings.

Production of documents

In certain countries the law empowers conciliators to compel the parties to produce documents in conciliation proceedings. What has been said above concerning the conciliator's attitude as regards the power to compel the parties' attendance is also applicable here. In other words, the conciliator should try to secure the voluntary production of documents, and should avoid as far as possible any resort to compulsion.

With regard to interest disputes he should consider the use of compulsion in connection with a joint conference only at the insistence of one of the parties. The situation is different in the case of other types of dispute where the issues involve questions of fact. But even in those cases the conciliator must not forget that he cannot issue a binding decision but can only promote a voluntary settlement. Moreover, it is possible that those cases, or most of them, can be brought before the ordinary courts or before labour arbitration tribunals with power to make binding decisions. If so, and if the document in question is of material importance and his request for its production goes unheeded, it may be best for the conciliator to desist from any further effort so that the matter can be brought immediately before the court or tribunal.[1]

Conciliator's case preparation for individual meetings

The conciliator must fully prepare himself for every meeting with the parties. He will adjust his preparations to the objectives he has in mind for the meeting in question. Like so many other aspects of the conciliation

---

[1] This is an exception to the suggestion made on p. 26 that the conciliator should not allow himself to be deterred by the possibility that a dispute may be referred to arbitration.

process, the manner of making these preparations is essentially a matter of personal style. However, in as far as it is a question of orderly organisation of work, the following principles may be suggested :

- The conciliator should always make certain that the case file folder is in his possession. A properly maintained folder will have the most current, appropriate memoranda on top, and all pertinent notes, reports, and correspondence easily available in an orderly, chronological arrangement ; research material compiled by the conciliator should also be in the folder so that it is readily available.

- Regardless of the frequency with which the conciliator has been meeting the parties, he should review his files before a meeting to establish firmly in his own mind all the relevant points. This is even more necessary when the conciliator has a number of pending assignments ; in moving from one case to another he can easily forget distinctions between the positions of the parties in different cases. The parties' negotiators will become quite distressed if the conciliator must be frequently informed of recent developments and reminded how matters stand. Their particular dispute is most important to them, and they believe it should be of prime concern to the conciliator assigned to the case. A conciliator reminding the negotiators, rather than being reminded by them, will secure their respect, attention and co-operation.

- In preparing for a meeting it is helpful for the conciliator to divide his review into three parts, namely the unresolved issues remaining before the parties ; the present position of each side on each of those issues, and the rationale for such positions ; and possibilities of accommodation, if any, in respect of each. Information on the third point may be a combination of what has been said and of the implications the conciliator has drawn from previous discussions.

CONDUCT OF MEETINGS

7

The conciliator is always striving to make each meeting as productive as possible. It is imperative that the procedural side of meetings be easily and artfully handled. This will minimise the diversion of the conciliator's attention from the substantive portion of his responsibilities. While for experienced conciliators the conduct of meetings becomes second nature, careful planning and execution are required on the part of those who are less experienced. In this chapter certain guidelines are suggested for the conduct of joint conferences and separate meetings, and it is hoped that on that basis, and by modifying the guidelines to meet his own requirements, a conciliator can develop a technique suited to his abilities.

This account is based on the assumption that the dispute is difficult to settle. In some cases, however, the conciliator may find that the parties show at an early stage a disposition to be reasonable and to compromise. He may then restrict his participation to guiding the discussions and encouraging the parties to put forward their own solutions. The conciliator may contribute to the settlement of the dispute simply by his presence at meetings, although he will if necessary convey a proposed solution from one party to the other while they are separated, and may assist in producing a formula embodying a mutually acceptable proposition.

In relatively minor disputes, too, the conciliator's intervention may be limited to holding separate meetings with the two parties. He may be able by such meetings to arrange a settlement which the management will agree to implement immediately, so that there will be no need for any further action on his part. In other circumstances he may succeed in bringing about substantial agreement, and may bring the parties together only for the signing of the agreement or to thresh out the remaining minor issues. Here again, the conciliator's presence can be invaluable.

JOINT CONFERENCES

Greetings and preliminary discussions

When a joint conference is to be held the conciliator should be ready to meet the parties on their arrival at the meeting place. Promptness is generally accepted as a reflection of interest in a dispute, as well as of a desire to deal with the problem quickly. Most importantly, from the conciliator's point of view, in some countries it counters the unmerited charge that government officials lack interest in their work. Arrival in advance also provides an opportunity to make certain that the material facilities required for the meeting are in order.

The conciliator should be certain of the names of those whom he will be meeting, and of their respective organisational functions. This is not difficult with regard to the persons to whom he has addressed the invitation to the meeting. He can also obtain from them in advance or during the initial contacts information as regards the other members of the negotiating committees. The conciliator should acknowledge the presence of each and every member of the negotiating committees individually : he should not direct his attention only to the committee members whom he considers important, since if he does so the other members of a committee may feel slighted ; in their own eyes they occupy a position of status in their organisations regardless of what their actual role may be at the bargaining table. By a handshake or other customary individual greeting, the conciliator can show his awareness of their status and his personal respect for each of them.

Usually the parties do not arrive at the meeting place at the same time. This is another reason for the conciliator to arrive early, and for having adequate meeting facilities. With a joint conference room and one or more separate session rooms the conciliator can assign the parties to waiting rooms until the opening of the joint meeting. Also, one of the parties, on arrival, may request a discussion with the conciliator before the joint conference begins. Incidentally, when this occurs the conciliator should inform the other party of the request for separate discussion. If possible the waiting party should be informed of the approximate duration of the discussion.

From time to time one side may wish to hold a closed meeting—closed even to the conciliator—before the start of a joint conference. This is not out of the ordinary ; there are a host of reasons why a group may make a request for a closed meeting. For example, there may be members of the committee who were not able to attend a prior strategy meeting by the group. Whatever the reason, the conciliator should be able to comply with such requests.

Introductions and seating

The face-to-face confrontation of the joint conference can have its share of awkward moments. The conciliator can avoid the uneasiness, particularly at the initial meeting, by keeping the parties separated until he decides that they are ready to meet. At that time he should personally accompany the parties to the joint conference room. He should then casually suggest that each side's spokesman or chief member make the introductions to the other side. This, of course, is not necessary in subsequent meetings, unless a new member is included in a committee. If the parties have previously attended joint conferences, the conciliator can dispense with the introductions by stating that he assumes everyone knows everyone else. If that is not the case, it should be a relatively easy matter to have new committee members made known to all.

Seating arrangements depend on the size of the negotiating committees. If the committees are large and there is a long conference table, the two committees will have to be seated on opposite sides of the table, with the chief spokesmen directly opposite each other at the centre. If all the members of the committees cannot be seated at the table because it is not big enough, the conciliator should suggest a second line of chairs placed directly behind those at the table on the respective sides.

However, the presence of a large audience can be an embarrassment, as there may be a tendency for the leaders to speak to the gallery or to make protracted speeches with a view to impressing the back-benchers. This difficulty may be overcome by having only the leaders in the joint meeting and providing separate rooms for the other representatives. The leaders can retire to those rooms for consultations when the need arises. It is, however, essential to obtain the agreement of those concerned before such an arrangement can be resorted to.

When negotiating committees are small and consist, for example, of not more than five members each, seating arrangements are simpler. In such cases the spokesmen should usually be seated near the conciliator at the head of the table. The two committees are seated on their respective sides of the table in whatever way each group has decided.

Whatever the size of the committees and the alignment of the committee members, the conciliator takes his seat at the head of the table as chairman of the meeting.

Opening statements and presentation of cases

It is a truism that the less said by the conciliator at the opening of a joint conference the better. He should open by a brief statement welcoming the parties and thanking them for answering his request to attend the meeting. Even under laws requiring the parties' attendance at conciliation proceedings the conciliator would do well to make the same opening. The conciliator will then indicate briefly his understanding of the dispute as obtained by him from the initial contacts with the parties He should avoid involving himself in a lengthy or detailed analysis of the dispute, since this can lead to immediate arguments on points of detail with either side, which is a waste of time and gets the meeting off to a bad start.

However, where the parties have not previously had any experience of conciliation proceedings the conciliator should amplify his opening statement to include an explanation of the objective of conciliation, the purpose of the meeting and the procedure that will be followed. He should emphasise that a dispute is only an incident in the continuing relations between the employer and his labour force or between the parties in collective bargaining. As long as an employer carries on his enterprise, he maintains a standing relationship with his labour force, although the employment of any individual worker may from time to time be terminated for one reason or another. Once a collective bargaining relationship has been established it tends to be permanent, and will normally cease only when the union concerned is replaced by another union as the workers' bargaining representative. As often emphasised by observers of labour relations, an industrial dispute cannot be approached in the same way as a court case, which generally involves parties between whom there is no contractual relationship (or whose contractual relationship has come to an end). In the case of an industrial dispute the parties will continue to work together under the terms of the settlement by which the dispute is terminated. Not only will a conciliator need to bear this fact in mind himself ; it is also his essential task to impress it clearly and indubitably upon the parties, and to persuade them to make it the hallmark of their discussions.

Even when he has explained the objective of conciliation, the purpose of the meeting and the procedure that will be followed during his initial contacts with the parties, it is still desirable that the conciliator should repeat his explanations, in the presence of both parties, in his opening statement. It should be remembered, however, that conciliation proceedings are not supposed to involve lectures, and that this is true even when conciliation is a novel experience for both parties. The conciliator's statement can be limited to the brief time available by concentrating on the objective of the conciliation service and the parties' responsibilities for solving their problem.

To make certain that the parties are ready the conciliator should then state that he has finished his introductory remarks and that he will respond to questions, if any. He should say this in a way that shows that he would like to be of assistance and is not merely fulfilling a formality.

Having made his opening statement, the conciliator calls on one side or the other to present its case. In general, the party that has put forward the unsatisfied claims or taken the action or decision leading to the dispute should be allowed to speak first. In practice, in interest disputes this is nearly always the trade union.

The opening statement will be made by the spokesman of the side concerned, who is normally the leader of the negotiating committee. At the conclusion of his statement he may call on his colleagues to make corroborative statements on matters of which they have detailed knowledge. The conciliator will then ask the spokesman of the other side to present his case and reply to the points made by the opposite party. The latter spokesman may similarly call on his colleagues to amplify upon and corroborate his statements. The cases of the two sides having thus been presented, the usual course is then to allow a general debate between the parties.

The above procedure may also be followed in disputes arising from a comprehensive set of demands or proposals. In those cases, however, it may be desirable to have at the beginning a fairly complete picture of the unresolved issues, and the conciliator may therefore consider an alternative procedure : this consists in his asking the side which put forward the claims to make a concise listing, in easily identifiable items, of the matters that call for a decision. This initial listing has the dual purpose of acquainting the conciliator with the problems and of allowing a check by the parties of the list of undecided issues.

There will be a great inclination on the part of the side reciting the listing to slip into an argument of the issues, and an equally strong inclination on the opposite side to be quick to respond in kind. This should be avoided, and the parties should be given to understand that the listing is not a matter for debate and that they will have ample opportunities to expand their respective views later on.

After the listing has been completed, the conciliatior should ask the other side whether the list as given is complete. Here again, the party to which the query is put should be requested to answer that question only and not to advance arguments. Should there be disagreement, the conciliator can get the discussion going by stating that agreement need not be reached on a list distinguishing between issues that are still open and those that have been settled : the principal aim at this stage is to have all three parties at the table see the full agenda before them.

The next step is for each side to clarify its position on each issue. Where there are accompanying position papers, charts or fact sheets the conciliator should request a copy. Further, it should be an accepted courtesy in negotiations to provide the opposite side with copies of informative material supporting a declared position. It is desirable that the clarification should continue without questions or interruption by the conciliator or the listening party. Once the clarification by one side has been made, the conciliator must allow for questions by the other side, and he may have his own questions to ask. The conclusion of the clarification of the parties' stand on the issues sets the stage for a general debate between the two sides.

Chairmanship

In the course of this debate it is common form for each side to challenge the accuracy of the other's statements, to endeavour to establish facts in support of its position and to demand answers to questions that are regarded as vital issues. The role of the conciliator during this debate is again to say as little as possible himself. The speakers on each side should normally be expected to address each other through the chairman. This is, however, a matter of discretion, according to the prevailing circumstances.

One of the main tasks of the conciliator is to keep the parties attentive to the main purpose, to control the discussion so that it is carried on in an orderly manner and so as to avoid irrelevancies as far as possible, and to call for restraint if the discussion becomes overheated and if an element of bad temper or personal abuse enters into the proceedings. This is rather easy to say but the fact is that the concilator's role in guiding and controlling the discussion is an extremely delicate one. He will often have to ask himself how much control he should exercise.

Intense and intemperate exchanges may be expected. While they may serve a purpose, as an outlet for bitter feelings, there must at some point be a restraint on harsh words, abusive language or violent gestures. The conciliator will be guided by local rules of etiquette in judging whether behaviour at the conference table has gone far beyond permissible limits. There is also probably a test which he can apply in determining how far he can allow the parties to go on with behaviour which may seem to be offensive : as long as it does not bring either party to the point of staging a walk-out or breaking off the negotiations, he may not need to intervene. It can be assumed that there is joint recognition that behaviour otherwise offensive is an accepted part of negotiating activity, but the conciliator will always need to keep his senses keenly alerted to any signs of danger in the parties' reactions.

Another main task of the conciliator at the joint conference is to listen. It is by carefully listening to the debate between the parties and watching their behaviour that he can best assess the real facts of the dispute, their stand on the issues and any changes in their attitude. The opening statement of each side will have been carefully prepared, and may seem in isolation to present an irrefutable case ; but when these statements are subjected to examination, criticism and questioning by the other side, the weaknesses within them become apparent. It is important that no limitations should be applied that can create the feeling that the parties have not been allowed to substantiate their case fully and to make all the points and ask all the questions which they wish to put. The conciliator must therefore listen attentively to the discussions between the two sides—without giving any sign of impatience, irritation or boredom—even if the discussion appears to him to be unnecessarily repetitive.

The degree of formality at joint meetings depends on national practice, including the influence of legal tradition, and also varies according to the circumstances. In a meeting at which a large number of representatives are present the conciliator may need to exercise more control over the discussion, and the proceedings may thus tend to become more formal than when a meeting is smaller. In certain countries the practice has been to keep the proceedings as informal as possible, and experience has shown that this normally produces quite satisfactory results. Informality should not, however, be carried to a point at which the discussion loses coherence and strays from the main purpose of the meeting; it is the conciliator's job to prevent this from happening.

If he has to call any side to order, or to caution against offensive language or interrupt irrelevant discussion, he should do so courteously and in the most tactful language he can employ; otherwise he may lay himself open to a charge, which most likely will remain unspoken, of being biased against the party concerned.

It is while acting as chairman of a joint meeting that the conciliator is required to exercise the utmost care to protect his impartiality. Above all, he must not criticise any side, or any stand or view expressed by either side. This is a fatal mistake which young and inexperienced conciliators often make.

The conciliator must be completely neutral and he must not express views that would strengthen the position of one side, i.e. on the soundness or otherwise of any argument put forward by either side or on whether the supporting data advanced by one side are more reliable than those presented by the other side. It is not possible to enumerate what a conciliator must not do during a joint meeting to avoid the possibility of either party's suspecting his impartiality : not only words but also gestures can constitute evidence of bias in favour of one side or the other. If in doubt he should reserve what he would like to say for the separate meetings.

SEPARATE MEETINGS

While the guidelines suggested in the following paragraphs are mainly concerned with separate meetings held in connection with a joint conference, they can also be applied to separate meetings of the Rhodes formula type of conciliation, where the conciliator's movements follow the same pattern. The suggested guidelines can also be applied with suitable adjustments to separate meetings with the parties at different times and places.

The call for separate meetings

A joint conference may result in an agreement. This happens seldom, and usually in very simple cases only, at the beginning of the conciliator's intervention. The debate between the parties will give the conciliator some idea of his chances, and of what further efforts he will need to make if he is to achieve a settlement. He may consider that he can make better progress by suspending the debate, meeting the parties separately and bringing them together again in a joint meeting.

There are various other reasons why the conciliator may find it desirable to hold separate meetings with the parties. As indicated earlier, his guiding principle will be to call for the type of meeting that will best serve his purpose at a given moment. The debate at the joint meeting may have given him a lead which he can more usefully or effectively pursue at a separate meeting. He may need to call off a bitter, acrimonious discussion and allow for some time for tempers to calm down in separate discussions with the parties. For the parties themselves and for the conciliator, a call for separate meetings, possibly preceded by closed meetings, may be a welcome respite from excessively repetitive, fruitless and tiring argumentation.

When the conciliator has made up his mind he informs the parties that the joint meeting is being suspended or adjourned and that he would like to meet them separately. Unless one or the other side asks him to meet them first, the decision is for him to make and he will primarily be guided by his purpose in wishing to have separate meetings. Generally speaking, too much importance should not be attached to this point, although he should avoid giving any appearance of having any special motive in seeing one party first. Unless his purpose dictates otherwise, the course which is perhaps least likely to cause adverse reaction is to meet first the side which has presented the initial demands or claim. Also, in the course of the joint meeting he may have formed the impression that one side has more to contribute towards reaching a compromise, and he may therefore consider that progress might be accelerated by seeing that party first. If there are two separate meeting rooms, he will conduct the parties to their respective rooms, going first with the party that will have to wait ; otherwise he asks the waiting party to stay in the joint meeting room and he conducts the other party to the other room.

Atmosphere and procedure

Much of the usefulness of this type of meeting, as compared with the joint conference, is due to its more informal atmosphere. The conciliator should avoid any conduct on his part that will minimise this informal air ; he should rather encourage it. His tone should be more casual and conversational ; his posture and the positioning of his chair should reflect a relaxed, but not unconcerned attitude. The aim of all this is to encourage on the part of participants an attitude more conducive to an open and reasonable discussion of problems, as opposed to the very defensive or aggressive stances that they usually assume at the joint meeting.

The question of where he should place himself at the meeting is relevant to the maintenance of its atmosphere of informality. His positioning should reflect the fact that he is a member of a group seeking to solve a problem, and is not carrying over into the meeting his role as chairman of the joint conference. He should not take a seat at the table on the side opposite the party present, as if he were occupying a place where the other party sat or would be. He should, if at all, take a seat that physically places him on the same side as those present ; this may not assure him of being looked upon as "one of us", but it at least lessens the chance of his being regarded as a member of the opposition.

There are two things that the conciliator should make clear to the side he is meeting : first, he will keep absolutely confidential any information that they may wish to give him in confidence; secondly, any exchange with him does not create a firm commitment, unless such a commitment is expressly stated.

In accordance with his purpose the conciliator may follow the same initial procedural steps as at the joint meeting. He may request a clarification of position and may similarly ask for a listing, in a straightforward manner, of unsettled issues. He may find that, in the absence of the other party, the presentation is different, not only in tone but also possibly as regards details, from that made previously at the joint conference ; he should be quick to note the differences or changes, because they will constitute some of his most valuable clues to the direction his further efforts should take.

The conciliator can provoke a more detailed explanation and further discussion by asking questions or making comments and suggestions. He pursues his objective by a more determined effort to probe into the party's attitude, for points in respect of which positions can be altered. His aim is to induce the participants to speak freely and spontaneously, and to shed as much as possible the belligerent attitudes they had at the joint meeting.

There will possibly be an effort to explain the other side's point of view. The conciliator should be prepared for this, and it should not be entirely discouraged. It is another source of information and does not commit the other party, which will have its turn to explain its attitude.

There are certain dangers that the conciliator must guard against in the separate meeting. Even in the absence of the other party, he needs to maintain and protect his impartiality. He should not criticise the absent party before the party he is meeting.

The conciliator should build up a stock of amiable but non-committal rejoinders which he can use when he is being drawn into a conversation on the weaknesses or deficiencies of the absent party. The party present may be encouraged to do this because of the informality and even intimacy of the separate session. Whether or not his views are purposely sought, the conciliator should not make any derogatory remarks concerning the other side.

In holding separate discussions with the parties, the conciliator will be conveying the views and attitudes of one party to the other. He should do so in such a way as to make it clear that such views and attitudes are not his own but those of the other side, and that he is presenting them on the latter's behalf to enable a full understanding of the situation to be obtained.

The conciliator should not be lulled into thinking that because of the absence of the other party a separate meeting is devoid of emotion. In the parties' face-to-face confrontation at the joint conference, there is always the other side as the target for one side's feelings of resentment or hostility. These feelings may not immediately or completely subside at the separate meeting, and the conciliator may be the only target against whom they can be directed. This is a fate which the conciliator must be prepared to accept. If the participants concerned are determined to agitate, perhaps it is better that their attention should be directed to the conciliator ; there is little danger that he will react in kind or will call for a cessation of the negotiations ; and he can take it good-naturedly.

It will often be found that progress in separate discussions is very slow owing to the reluctance of the parties to make concessions at an early stage and their desire to see whether any proposals are forthcoming from the other side before they make any move themselves. The conciliator must therefore be prepared to be extremely patient and to move between the two sides over a long period, often spending a substantial time with each in endeavouring to bring their attitudes and positions closer to each other.

QUESTIONS CONCERNING BOTH KINDS OF MEETING

There are certain features and problems that are common to the conduct of joint conferences and separate meetings, although the conciliator would generally have to give more attention to them in relation to joint conferences.

Record of proceedings

Except in cases where it is a matter of national practice, the taking of shorthand notes or tape recordings of conciliation proceedings should be discouraged. Quite apart from considerations of economy, it is undesirable because it will give an unnecessarily formal character to the proceedings and discourage free exchanges. Moreover, the existence of such records always entails the risk that many things said in confidence may become public property.

The conciliator can usually be relied on to take any necessary notes. It is often helpful for him to be accompanied by an assistant who can make brief notes on important points during the progress of the discussions. The assistant may note down a point and draw his attention to an aspect which he may have missed owing to his deep involvement in the discussion, but it must be made clear to the parties that the assistant has nothing else to do with the conduct of the meetings.

Order of discussion of the issues

When a dispute involves a number of issues the conciliator will have to decide on the order in which they will be discussed. It will always be desirable for the conciliator to consult the parties about their wishes in the matter. One way is to discuss the issues in the chronological order in which they originally came up. Another way is to begin by discussing first the more simple issues on which agreement will be easier to obtain. An agreement on an issue can create a favourable atmosphere for the discussion of the other issues.

It is a useful practice to put agreements reached on various issues in writing. However, the conciliator should not overlook the inter-relationship between the various issues : in many cases agreement on one issue in the course of the discussion may be regarded by the parties as tentative, subject to final agreement on all issues. This way of proceeding will allow the parties, in certain circumstances, to go back and reopen the discussion on clauses already agreed, as a means of setting off one concession against another.

The discussion of the issues may also proceed on the basis of a package deal. After the initial presentations and general debate one side or the other may formulate a combination of proposals which it offers as a basis for settlement. The combination of proposals is the "package" which usually includes wage increases and other benefits of monetary value. The total cost of a package is computed, and the computation will show that a specified amount of increase would be applied partly to rates of pay and partly to the financing of other monetary or fringe benefits. Thus the package offered by one side will show the priorities it attaches to the various items and the possible concessions it aims to obtain. During the negotiations either side may propose more than one package, in which the modified items may represent concessions offered to the other side.

Duration of meetings

The duration of meetings varies enormously, and depends upon the complexity and urgency of the dispute and the attitudes of the parties. In general, it is desirable to allow as much time as possible, because enforced haste is not conducive to a good atmosphere for conciliation, and the parties will tend to resist being pushed to discuss in a hurry matters which they regard as of great importance.

The conciliator will find that an over-speedy settlement tends to be regarded with suspicion, on the ground that one or the other side has given up too easily the fight for better terms and concessions. Experienced negotiators prefer to proceed with due form and deliberation in what is sometimes described as the "ritual dance", and they expect the conciliator to play his part accordingly.

Sometimes keeping the parties together will ensure that progress is made, whereas at other times it can only aggravate the situation and a recess is necessary. With regard to separate meetings and the Rhodes formula, the conciliator can go back and forth from one side to another; he can avoid having to keep one party waiting too long, or inform the party that is waiting of the probable duration of his meeting with the other.

Adjournment

Except in very simple cases, more than one meeting is generally necessary before conciliation proceedings are concluded. In the case of a dispute involving the negotiation of a long and complicated agreement, a series of meetings may be held extending over weeks and even months.

Where there is need for further conciliation, the following procedure is suggested for adjourning a joint conference :

● If the conciliator has been meeting the parties separately, they should be brought together in the conference room to agree on the adjournment, unless extreme hostility makes it undesirable to seek a joint expression of agreement even on a purely procedural point such as this. Obviously, a meeting for this purpose is unnecessary if the request or suggestion for adjournment is made at a joint meeting.

● The conciliator should give a brief summary of the results of the meetings that have just taken place. At the same time the parties should provide each other with concise summaries of their respective positions on issues that remain outstanding.

● The date, time and place of the next meeting should be arranged, if possible. Alternatively, it may be suggested that the conciliator will be in touch with the parties, and that he will set another meeting date on the basis of his evaluation of the progress of the discussions.

● Appreciation should be expressed to both sides for participating in the meeting.

● Official adjournment should then be announced. It may be preceded, if appropriate, by a succinct statement, which should be a concise summing up of the conciliator's view, and should not contain any element of blame for anyone even if the discussions have not proceeded satisfactorily.

A meeting that concludes with an agreement between the parties leading to a settlement of the dispute requires a few elementary steps by the conciliator :

● The parties should be brought into a joint conference and a statement should be made on the issues that have been settled in the course of the meetings that have just taken place. It is generally desirable to put down the final settlement in writing, and to have the document initialled or signed by the parties. If a long agreement is involved and its drafting may take some time the parties may decide to meet again for the signing of the agreement. On the other hand, if the parties have a good working relationship the formality of signing a written agreement may be omitted.

● The conciliator should express appreciation for the co-operation of the parties, even when the meetings preceding the final agreement have been difficult or exhausting.

● He should make a clear statement that the conciliation proceedings are ended.

Press statements

The relationship between the conciliator and the parties to a dispute, on the one hand, and press, radio and television reporters on the other can be a very difficult one and call for careful handling if unfortunate consequences are to be avoided. It is not suggested, of course, that this applies to all or even the majority of disputes, because so many arise from issues that are of little interest to the press and other news media. Others, however, particularly those affecting essential services of various kinds or which for other reasons have an element of drama or news value, attract the full glare of publicity. This is a situation which has to be accepted and dealt with in such a way as to do the minimum damage to the negotiations in progress. Journalists have a job to do in gathering all the information they can obtain on any subject that is regarded as possessing news value. They are tenacious in pursuing this objective, and little is to be gained—in fact considerable harm can be done—by attempts to frustrate them.

On the other hand, press statements by the parties can be detrimental to the success of conciliation, especially if they reflect attitudes from which it will be difficult to retreat without loss of face. As is often the case in the field of international diplomacy, delicate negotiations cannot be conducted on the basis of making every move public and consequently exposed to uninformed criticism and comment. For example, after lengthy discussions a compromise solution may be reached, which the union leaders consider it necessary to put before their members for approval before they can agree to it as part of the settlement. This may be done at a meeting the following day or even some days later, but if the terms of the proposed compromise are disclosed to the press and revealed in the newspapers before the meeting, it can be taken as axiomatic that there is no more certain way of ensuring their rejection. This is not only because an opportunity is given possibly to a militant minority element to whip up opposition in advance but because there is a general and by no means unreasonable dislike among trade unionists of being informed of such matters through any source other than their accredited representatives.

The attitude to be adopted towards the press must therefore depend very much on the circumstances. When a series of meetings are held and reporters are seeking to obtain news of what has transpired in the course of each, it is generally desirable that the conciliator should seek the agreement of the parties to issue only a non-committal statement, e.g. to the effect that the meeting has taken place, that there has been a frank exchange of views, that progress has been made and that a further meeting has been arranged. This type of notice is frequently prepared by the conciliator, but he should always secure the approval of both sides to its contents and an undertaking that they will not say more themselves to the waiting reporters. Sometimes, such an undertaking is not observed by one of the individuals concerned and unauthorised information consequently appears. There is little that can be done about this, but fortunately it will be found that these occurrences are rare.

When a settlement has been reached and there is no necessity for the parties to seek ratification from their members, there is in general no objection, if the parties are willing, to disclosing the terms of the settlement immediately. When ratification is essential, however, the press notice can reveal that a provisional settlement has been reached and that the terms will be put to the membership concerned as quickly as possible. It is not possible to envisage every circumstance that can arise, but enough has been said to indicate the care that is necessary in dealing with this difficult problem.

Sometimes when a dispute is over the press ask for information on what took place during the course of the conciliation meetings, and at that stage it is often possible for the conciliator, with the agreement of the parties, to give an account of the various stages of the discussions as background information. He should of course be very discreet in the details he gives, and should avoid putting either of the parties in an unfavourable light. It is preferable to make some sort of statement whenever possible, because otherwise the press may speculate on the course of events and there is then a risk that it may produce a garbled and distorted account bearing little resemblance to the facts.

THE SEQUENTIAL PATTERN
OF CONCILIATION

8

It needs to be repeated that the function of the conciliator in a dispute is to help the parties towards an amicable settlement, and that the responsibility for determining the terms of the settlement rests primarily on the parties. In practical terms, his central objective is to reduce the differences between the parties to a point where the possibility of settlement arises. He has to accept at the outset that he is confronted with a situation of deadlock, since the differences that gave rise to the dispute will nearly always have been the subject of previous discussion between the parties. He has therefore to consider carefully the means he can adopt to break that deadlock and find scope for accommodation and possible compromise. Skilful handling of meetings, discussed in the preceding chapter, is one of the means by which the conciliator moves towards his main objective. Various aspects of the conciliator's substantive responsibility for leading the parties to agreement are discussed in greater detail in the present chapter.

As indicated earlier, no two cases can possibly be exactly alike : there will be differences in the facts, the issues, the parties involved and their personalities and attitudes. The slightest difference in shading or degree can require the conciliator to take an approach different from any that he has tried before. The dissimilarities between cases and the need for the conciliator to adopt in each case an approach appropriate to its particular circumstances do not detract from the fact that there is a certain over-all pattern to the conciliation process.

This pattern may be better understood by reference to the process of bilateral collective bargaining. When they have already had some experience of collective bargaining the parties are often able to reach agreements by themselves. All over the world thousands of collective agreements are negotiated every year in this way without resort to industrial action. This process of unassisted negotiations falls into three major phases.

During the initial phase of the negotiations the parties are usually adamant in upholding their respective positions. Sooner or later, after some discussion, a second phase begins with a softening of the parties' initial attitudes. This phase may be initiated when one party adopts a more conciliatory tone which is reciprocated by the other. Whatever the causative factor, the parties may be said during this phase to enter into a mood for accommodation. This mood is converted, during the third phase, into a positive search for possible terms of compromise.

The process of conciliation generally follows a sequence which is essentially similar to that described above, likewise consisting of three major phases. However, there are at least two significant differences.

In the first place, the parties come to conciliation as adversaries in an openly declared dispute. They are therefore likely to appear before the conciliator with more hardened attitudes. The initial phase of the conciliation process may thus be described as one of "hard posture".

Secondly, during conciliation each party will be primarily concerned with protecting its bargaining position. Neither party normally takes the initiative in adopting a conciliatory or accommodating attitude. It becomes the important task of the conciliator to induce the parties into such an attitude. The second phase becomes a search for accommodation on the part of the conciliator.

In both processes the third phase may be described as that in which the parties are in the mood for settlement or compromise, the major difference being, of course, that during the conciliation process the presence of the conciliator provides an additional source of suggestions that can lead to a settlement of the dispute.

It is important for the conciliator to understand the sequential pattern of conciliation because it can guide his moves, especially as regards timing. The attitudes and behaviour of the parties differ in each phase, and the conciliator must adjust his moves accordingly. It must be emphasised, however, that the phases do not follow each other in a neatly observable pattern or simply in numerical order. The phases correspond to attitudes ; and it will be realised that from time to time, even in the course of ultimately successful negotiations, the attitudes of one or both parties may momentarily become less conciliatory. There is therefore no precise point at which one phase definitely ends and another commences ; in particular the intermediate phase does not run its full course without overlapping with the others. None the less the conciliator will sense the general long-term trend of the negotiations irrespective of transitory fluctuations in the attitudes of the parties.

HARD POSTURE

The hard posture that the parties generally assume during the initial phase of conciliation may be shown in a number of ways—inflexibility, adamant defence of position, efforts to discredit the other side, out-of-hand rejection of opposing views, pointing to extreme examples for support. During this phase each party invariably considers that it is wholly right and the other side wholly unreasonable or wholly wrong ; neither party can see or will admit any merit in any argument or proposition put forward by the other side. There may be not only antagonism but open hostility between the parties.

The hard posture is not always or necessarily displayed in a blatant or flamboyant manner. It can be expressed with a muted firmness which is no less pronounced, and to which it is more difficult for the conciliator to respond, than the more obvious signs. Instead of verbal assaults or expressive gestures, there may just be a studied coolness or stiffness in one party's relationship with the other ; comments may be made as if the other party were not even present.

It will be useless for the conciliator to take any initative which the parties are in no mood to accept. For the conciliator the phase of hard posture is therefore essentially a time of muffled action. He plays a relatively passive role by comparison with the initiatives he can take during the other phases. This is mainly a time for listening, observing, gathering information on the negotiators and the issues and planning his future course of action.

If there are heated arguments his primary interest is to keep the parties talking without reaching the point of breaking off the negotiations. The parties will be in a combative mood ; he has to adopt an oblique approach in his efforts to lessen tensions and bring reason to the bargaining table ; there is a danger that he himself may be attacked ; and he has to be careful about the way he asks questions or makes observations.

Nothwithstanding his relatively passive role, this is a valuable phase for the conciliator. From the parties' declarations and the exchanges between them as well as from his own inquiries, he can obtain a fuller sense of the situation as a whole, of the parties' positions and of the gap which separates them, and on that basis he can plan his future moves. During this phase he may begin his efforts, particularly during separate meetings, to find out the parties' real attitudes on the issues, though it will invariably be necessary for him to continue these efforts in the succeding phase.

The duration of the hard posture phase depends on the circumstances of the case and the personalities. It may be relatively long, as in cases in which several important or complicated issues are involved. The conciliator has to watch for signs that this phase is tailing off, at which time he can begin to assert his role in more active and positive ways.

SEARCH FOR ACCOMMODATION

In most cases, during the hard posture phase, the differences between the parties seem irreconcilable. The second major phase involves prising the parties from their original positions. The objective of the conciliator is to induce in them a mood in which they will be ready for accommodation, to persuade them to adopt more flexible attitudes and to move closer towards each other. Above all, he is concerned with preventing the discussions from developing into a stalemate which will spell the failure of his efforts.

This phase contains two sub-phases, namely first the development of an attitude of inquiry, and secondly the presentation of alternatives and evaluations. There is no clearly discernible demarcation between the two sub-phases, and they often overlap. In certain cases there may be a third sub-phase : the conciliation of intra-party differences. For the most part the activities of the conciliator discussed below are carried out in separate meetings.

Attitude of inquiry

As the parties' hard posture becomes less marked, the conciliator should stimulate an attitude of inquiry. This is the sub-phase in which he will aim at dislodging the parties from the positions in which they were entrenched when the conciliator took up the case.

The conciliator's efforts can now take two directions. One is to bring home to each party that its position is not actually as right or as perfect as it is claimed to be. The other is to let each party see that there is some merit in the other party's position ; this is also to encourage mutual appreciation by the parties of each other's point of view, which is an essential condition before they can be persuaded to bring their positions closer to each other.

This sub-phase is a very sensitive stage. In effect, the conciliator is challenging the parties' positions. Perhaps the safest opening wedge that can be tried is a series of well planned questions. By starting with questions, the conciliator avoids a direct and possibly hostile encounter with the parties. The manner of asking questions should show a desire to have more information, an interest in gaining more insight into the problem, and an intent to help. When a person is asked to give of his knowledge it is seldom that he will reject such a complimentary gesture. This will give the conciliator a foothold for his further moves.

In seeking to obtain changes in the parties' attitudes and position, the conciliator also wants them to start thinking in a more rational way; questions can be alternated with short statements that raise questions inferentially. The direct question is particularly helpful to learn about such matters as past disputes, working conditions, occupational structure and the tasks in a skilled trade. The purpose of an inferential or indirect question it to raise doubt in the mind of the listener, doubt concerning the accuracy or comprehensiveness of his information ; it can also suggest a possible flaw in his reasoning, an aspect of the matter which he has not considered, or the points of strength on the other side.

A technique closely related to asking questions is requesting a repetition of supporting arguments. The purpose of repeated explanation is to force the spokesman himself to listen to the arguments he is putting forward. There is a possibility that his presentation may begin to sound a bit less convincing, even to him. This takes time, and sometimes it is the only tool the conciliator has to work with. He may detect a change when the presentation is made with less fervour and enthusiasm than before.

It is rather natural that the parties should seek favourable endorsements by the conciliator of their respective stands on an issue. He can easily shield his reactions during the joint conference, and the matter is seldom pressed there. It is in the separate meetings that more insistent attempts to obtain his endorsement are usually made. He should at all costs resist such attempts and avoid being unwittingly drawn into making such endorsements. The least sign on his part that he takes a favourable view of a party's stand can make that party refuse to budge from its position.

It is not often that both parties will alter their positions simultaneously. The conciliator may aim to prevail upon one party to make the first movement ; this party will be the one that has shown a more softened attitude. If the conciliator succeeds in inducing one party to change its position, he will be in a better position to demand a reciprocal move by the other.

Each side weighs a different set of risks in remaining at deadlock. The conciliator must draw attention to the specific dangers of taking inflexible positions. The parties must be shown that accepting less than their original goals is preferable to not reaching any agreement whatever. Edging the parties toward the realisation that their demands and counter-demands are not going to be met in the form and manner desired calls for availability of alternatives, and moves the process into the next sub-phase.

Evaluation and presentation of alternatives

This is a sub-phase in which the conciliator must be ready with suggestions that are wholly or partly acceptable to the parties. He must be ready to function as an expert having a thorough grasp of the problems and having prepared the way for a settlement.

At this point, when the conciliator is encouraging a new train of thought, an analysis of the negotiations may be presented. This should attempt to cover the causes of the problem, a brief digest of where the parties stand, possible consequences of maintaining such positions, and a suggestion of what the conciliator may feel to be movement toward a viable alternative.

The intensity with which bargaining is commonly pursued serves to prevent the adversaries from occasionally stepping back from the heat of the discussions to pause for at least a temporarily detached view. This is a function that the conciliator can very well perform, especially since he has full control of the proceedings. It provides an occasion for the conciliator to state his evaluations.

They will be directed to a number of questions. Some will be asked by the parties themselves, others will be provoked by the state of negotiations. At any stage of the negotiations, when the conciliator finds it useful to state his evaluations, they must be on the basis of benefits to be gained. It is of absolutely no use either for the parties or for the conciliation process to submit evaluations on the basis of moral judgements. Rather, a purpose of an evaluation should be precisely to divert the parties from that type of thinking. The evaluation should demonstrate what each side may have already gained up to that point, and should especially highlight points of mutual benefit. On the other hand the evaluation may show that very little progress is being made and that the parties should make more serious efforts. It may also be possible to indicate a new approach.

The conciliator may consider trying to reduce the relative importance attached to certain demands. Lessening the value put on a demand may cause some loosening of the attachment to it. This is a very delicate matter. Negotiators who are just on the point of backing down a bit must be convinced that their personal values are not threatened. This is most often the case with less experienced negotiators, who tend to equate a reduction or easing of their demands with betrayal of their principles. Veterans of collective bargaining may also suffer the same pangs and require occasional bolstering. Just as individual negotiators show qualms about diminishing or withdrawing demands, so do committees as groups. The conciliator's appeal to the group is not unlike that to the individual. The committtee must see no threat to its unity, efforts and ultimate goals.

The conciliator is at the stage at which he will begin to face serious attacks as he moves from the passive role of listening and questioning to a more active role. The parties will be willing to change positions only when realistic alternative solutions are advanced ; at the same time, no leadership wants to abdicate responsibility. This is really a period full of pitfalls. The conciliator's abilities will be strained to the utmost as he attempts to persuade one of the parties to accept changes without feeling that it has lost control over the conduct of its own case.

The task of formulating and presenting counter-arguments, especially in separate meetings, will be familiar to conciliators. It is a key function, and the necessary attention paid to a number of points will facilitate its performance :

- Counter-arguments have much more credibility when proffered in a form and context not anticipated by the listeners.
- Counter-arguments must be submitted at a time when they will be most persuasive. Improperly timed and improperly constructed, they can only increase resistance to later forceful representations.
- Counter-arguments that are repetitious in substance will run headlong into previously erected resistance. The conciliator should avoid using stale rationale : it may be interpreted as a sign that he is at a dead end.

In the course of separate meetings, the conciliator will relay the position of one party to the other. When he presents the views of the other side he must be certain that he understands all the ramifications of an issue, and that his own exposition is clearly intelligible to his listeners. Here again, the conciliator must make the fullest use of his clarity of thought and expression.

When the parties have to listen to the conciliator, he should give them an opportunity to state their objections or support. In this way the conciliator can avoid committing himself too far, at the danger of later finding himself in a position from which he cannot gracefully withdraw. The conciliator should note the reaction of the group he is addressing : the substance of any objections will indicate what impression is being made.

The fact that a party has indicated its willingness to listen to guidance is no guarantee that the conciliator is on the way to a complete breakthrough. His suggestions will be minutely scrutinised by all those involved on one side, and he may find himself in the vortex of an intra-party controversy. This may have nothing to do with the conciliator personally or his suggestions. Generally it is more likely to mean that at that stage the negotiators have not lost all hopes of attaining their original objectives.

Conciliation of intra-party differences

The conciliation of intra-party differences is a sub-phase that receives little notice except from the conciliator. It demands considerable attention and requires great skill.

Such differences can come to light on either side, especially where trade unions and employers' organisations are concerned. Where bargaining takes place at the enterprise level the structure of management usually ensures that singleness of purpose will discourage countervailing forces ; on the other hand trade unions and employers' organisations are by their very nature more susceptible to internal struggles. The formation of a union, in particular, stems from a broad band of aspirations and grievances, real or imagined. The union must keep closed ranks among a body of workers which may include individuals skilled and unskilled, young and old, aggressive and non-aggressive and so forth. The union's base must of necessity be wide, and its demands usually reflect the varying needs of the membership. Hence there may not be full agreement within a union on certain items in the collection of claims put forward at the bargaining table. Differences within a union negotiating committee may also be due to internal union rivalries.

As the conciliator attempts to obtain changes in the party's position, withdrawal or downgrading of issues and modification of others, he is creating both adherents and antagonists within the committee. The cleavage may establish a number of factions or be limited to two major sides. Whatever occurs, the conciliator is now just as actively engaged in the intra-group struggle as he is in the inter-party conflict. The same difficulties as are present in the main arena are felt, and similar means may be employed to cope with them : in brief, it is a conciliation case within a conciliation case.

His awareness of the push and pull of the intra-party differences should make the conciliator especially careful and methodical in dealing with them. If he can elicit vocal opposition to his suggestions, and support for them, he stands a much better chance of overcoming his opponents. Otherwise, the submerged dissidence can be a constant source of difficulty.

The conciliator must gauge the strength of the faction taking issue with him. His main concern now is to ensure that changes in attitude within the two groups will keep up with the inter-group attitude. Without allowing any noticeable slowing down in the main negotiations, he must try to accelerate agreement among the opposing forces within each party.

A technique that can be effective in bringing recalcitrant committee members into line is to demonstrate that the group is arriving at a consensus. This is normally effective, but there will be cases when diehard dissidents will be unmoved by any effort.

This is another contingency in which the conciliator can act too quickly : group consensus has its greatest force when it evolves in the natural course of events. On the other hand, the conciliator must stand ready to point out what is taking place, should the committee be unaware that a consensus has been reached.

MOOD FOR SETTLEMENT

The third major phase of the conciliation process is the emergence of the appropriate mood for settlement. The main objective of the conciliator is to prod, encourage and assist the parties to make modified proposals and counter-proposals.

Words cannot describe how gingerly the conciliator must act in this phase. It may seem that the imagination which will have helped get the parties this far will have developed enough momentum to carry the disagreement to a satisfactory resolution. Unfortunately, however, the mood for settlement is like the waves of the sea : it can surge and recede very quickly. The conciliator who relaxes at this stage may well find himself in distress ; he must carefully nurse and actively foster the spirit of compromise on both sides.

A conciliator should not seek, or hope to obtain, sudden and dramatic moves by the negotiators. In a career of conciliation, the times when this happens will most likely be memorable occasions that can be counted on the fingers of one hand.

Negotiators can go to great lengths to mask their intentions. The conciliator must give sharp attention to both words and behaviour, to what is said and what is implied.

Probably the earliest sign that areas of agreement are within reach occurs when one side acknowledges that it understands the views expressed by the opposite side. This does not necessarily mean that there is ready agreement, but it is a sign of recognition, and is usually a forerunnner of an announced modification of previous positions.

Usually a friendlier tone can also be noted. This is a relative matter : for instance, where formerly there was an absence of direct communication across the bargaining table, there may now be a direct exchange of comments. That is an extreme example ; the point is that the conciliator should not be looking for an atmosphere that could be described as "friendly" by absolute standards.

Another indication of a closing of the gap between the parties is a partial or fragmentary acceptance of a proposal. Negotiators usually seek to avoid appearing too eager to settle, but at the same time do not want to do anything which might discourage flexibility on the other side ; therefore they sometimes seek refuge in a partially affirmative response.

The conciliator can get the parties over this hurdle by securing a committed response when the first move is ready to be made. A committed response is an affirmative reply by one party to a suggestion by the conciliator, which is contingent upon the other party's making a similar response or a corresponding movement. By arranging such a prior commitment the conciliator can assure the negotiators on one side that by going first they will not be weakening their position on some other point.

A more rapid pace in the negotiations will be perceptible as the parties find themselves concurring in suggestions and jointly preparing some terms of agreement. Compliance by one side with requests made by the other or by the conciliator is undoubtedly a good sign that the mood for settlement has a solid grip.

At this stage attention should be concentrated on the search for possible terms of compromise. Distractions from the main issues should now be dealt with quickly and with as much finality as possible. They include attempts to revive issues that have been disposed of, to raise new or secondary subjects that do not help to clarify the issues, or to test the negotiators of the other party to see how much fight remains in them. If possible the discussions, in joint or separate sessions, should be continued until final settlement is reached : if any postponement is allowed there is a danger that the mood of settlement so laboriously attained may fade away.

The conciliator encourages and assists the parties to develop their own proposed solutions—amended proposals and counter-proposals that can provide the basis for a compromise. He may participate in the discussions within a party's negotiating committee to select which of the various possible solutions put forward shall be proposed to the other side.

Ultimately, it may be necessary to resort to a conciliator's proposal. This, in effect, is a one-shot effort by the conciliator to put forward a final package deal which will resolve the dispute either on one item or over the whole range of disputed items.

The conciliator formally presents his proposal at a joint meeting. He must be certain that it will be accepted by both parties, because he cannot allow himself the luxury of making a second proposal. The greatest asset of a conciliator's proposal is its finality ; if a proposal is rejected a second one can also be rejected, likewise a third and so on. It is unthinkable for a conciliator to place himself in such a situation since he would inevitably lose credibility in the eyes of the parties.

The necessary groundwork must have been laid before the conciliator makes his proposal. It may be based on the committed responses which the two sides have previously made to him. Otherwise, he should make his proposal only once the parties' positions, as shown by their last amended proposals and counter-proposals, are close enough to provide a realistic possibility of settlement.

It is highly preferable, in order to be sure of joint acceptance, that the conciliator should clear his proposal in advance with each party before submitting it at a joint meeting.

CONCILIATION TECHNIQUES

9

The preceding chapter contains some discussion of the successive use of different conciliation techniques. In this chapter the subject of techniques as such, as a whole, will be treated in further detail. It is not possible, however, to indicate what particular techniques a conciliator should employ. The discussion below is simply intended to help the young conciliator in his general understanding of conciliation techniques. For the sake of clarity, certain points already brought out in previous chapters will be repeated here.

CONCILIATION AS AN ART

The dictionary defines "technique" as a "mood of artistic expression" or "manner of artistic performance". The term "conciliation techniques" has become commonplace, but whether this entails acceptance of the view that conciliation is essentially an art it is not possible to say. Nevertheless, the emphasis generally placed on experience as the only effective way of acquiring a sufficient mastery of conciliation techniques does suggest that conciliation has some characteristics of an art.

In the practice of conciliation we can speak of the art of listening, the art of asking questions, the art of timing, and above all the art of persuasion. There are also people who view conciliation as an art because a case is always a fresh challenge to a conciliator to employ and devise techniques suitable to its circumstances, and because no two conciliators will approach a dispute in exactly the same way.

Personal style

As he gains experience a conciliator will develop his own techniques. At the beginning he will be influenced by any previous training he may have had and by the advice of his more experienced colleagues. But while he may benefit and learn from the experience of others, his techniques will essentially depend on his own temperament and outlook. The conciliator's approach to the problems with which he is confronted is inevitably personal and individualistic. Although he operates in accordance with generally accepted broad principles, in any dispute situation his personality reacts to the facts of that situation and to the attitudes of other parties involved in it. From this it follows that no two conciliators are likely to handle the same dispute in exactly the same way and that the manner in which a conciliator performs his function is essentially a matter of personal style.

Conciliation techniques are as varied as the personalities of conciliators. Many conciliators rely upon a straightforward approach to the parties; others prefer to work in a more subtle and calculated manner. There are conciliators who are forcefully active in taking initiatives and those who play a relatively more passive or less aggressive role. Conciliators differ not only in the character of the initiatives that they take but also in the degree of formality or informality that they introduce into the proceedings and in their relationship with the parties.

One cannot be dogmatic concerning which particular styles are preferable. Success in the work of conciliation has not been limited to any particular style or type of personality of the conciliator. It is, however, important that the conciliator should act naturally and not in an artificial or visibly contrived manner, and his style must therefore conform to his personality. For example, a conciliator's effectiveness may be partly due to his ability to tell anecdotes, but an anecdote told by one conciliator may fall flat when told by another conciliator who has not the same talent.

Listening, asking questions and timing

A conciliator must listen attentively to the parties so that he can follow closely what they say. But his manner of listening is also important because it constitutes evidence of his own attitude which will affect the parties' attitude towards him. A skilful conciliator can show by the way he listens to the parties that he is fully interested in what they are saying and is trying hard to understand them. In spite of repetitions, digressions, irrelevances or long-winded declarations in which the parties may occasionally indulge, he should listen earnestly and sympathetically, without any sign of irritation, boredom or impatience.

A conciliator may ask questions to obtain information. When he does so for this purpose, his manner should not be that of an inquisitor, enforcement officer or legal cross-examiner. But questions are also used for other purposes : a question is a means of showing interest in what a person is saying ; it is a way of interrupting a speaker without the appearance of rudeness ; it is a vehicle for creating doubt in the mind of the speaker. It is also an indirect way of bringing home a point, and as such it may be preferable, in some circumstances, to a direct assertion.

It will be easy for a young conciliator to do the right thing at the wrong moment. He must think not only of doing the right thing but also of doing it at the right time. This requires effort, and it is only with experience that a conciliator acquires an almost instinctive sense of proper timing. There is a proper time for beginning active intervention in a dispute ; for calling joint conferences and separate meetings and for adjourning meetings ; for taking particular initiatives to break a stalemate in the negotiations ; for putting forward suggestions or proposals for a compromise.

Persuasion

The conciliator has no authority to impose a settlement on the parties, and can only try to persuade them to overcome their differences and agree upon a compromise. Three points may be noted.

(a) Understanding the parties

In the first place, as his aim is to bring reason and objectivity to the discussions, the conciliator will need to understand the causes which prevent a rational approach by the parties. In heated argumentation, they tend to be overcome by their emotions. The two sides also come to the bargaining table with their respective base of references. Both may use similar expressions, cite similar examples for support or advance similar statistical data, but their interpretations may bear little resemblance. Each side magnifies the negative aspects of the presentations of the other. An objective statement will be made to appear unacceptable by an attack on the manner in which the presentation was made, or the integrity of the spokesman may be called into question.

The course and climate of the negotiations can be affected by circumstances or happenings outside the bargaining table that bear no relation to the issues, such as a dismissal or reprimand of an employee, a quarrel between a supervisor and worker, or a proposed cutback in production which may entail lay-offs. A management which is dealing with a union for the first time will be influenced not only by what it considers to be the merits of the issues but also by its fears of what it believes a union to be capable of doing.

(b) Moral authority of the conciliator

Secondly, the possibilities for successful persuasion by a conciliator depends in a large measure on the way he is viewed by the parties. One or both of the parties may have been averse to his intervening. This negative reaction may not have been directed at him personally ; there may have merely been opposition to intervention by any outsider, whoever he might be. There are various possible reasons why a party to a dispute may not want conciliation by an outsider. If this was the kind of attitude which greeted a conciliator when he stepped into the dispute, he would be facing an impossible task of persuasion unless he could first bring about a reversal of that attitude. He would need to know the reason or reasons behind it. The situation just cited requires a special approach by the conciliator. More generally, the parties' attitude towards him will be determined by his personal attributes, behaviour and performance. Do they regard him as a reliable source of information and initiatives? Has he demonstrated attributes of impartiality, trustworthiness and expertise? The parties obtain an impression of him during his initial contacts with them ; it is confirmed, strengthened or modified during the subsequent stages of the proceedings.

A conciliator's ability to persuade the parties in a dispute will thus depend on the extent to which he has succeeded in winning their confidence in his ability to help them—in his impartiality, trustworthiness, and expertise. Expertise, as here used, goes beyond merely possessing a body of information ; the manner of utilising that information is really the key to being an accomplished conciliator.

(c) Marshalling pressures

There is, lastly, the question of the techniques of persuasion itself. A conciliator uses techniques of persuasion to achieve his object at a given moment—to induce either party to abandon a position, to induce either or both parties to make further steps towards each other, or to convince a party to accept a certain point of view, suggestion or proposal, or to agree to proposed terms of settlement.

If successful conciliators are asked what techniques of persuasion they employ, one may expect a wide variety of answers and explanations. If trade union and employers' representatives are asked what techniques have been effective in persuading them, one is also likely to receive a host of widely differing answers, but there is likely to be agreement on at least one point : that the task of persuasion in which the conciliator is engaged involves exerting pressure on one or both of the parties, or channelling it onto them, in order to obtain concessions for the settlement of their differences.

In any dispute the parties are usually subjected to a multiple reaction of different pressures. Some of those pressures are inherent in industrial disputes, others are created by the conciliator himself. They have been classified into three main forms : personal, social and political, and economic.[1]

Personal pressure originates from the conciliator. It is based on his personal relationship with the parties. Personal relationships and pressures are generally considered the mainstay of conciliation efforts. As techniques of persuasion, personal pressures may range from making a simple statement of fact to a detailed reasoning and exposition, from simple advice or suggestion to forceful advocacy and argumentation, from appeal to reason to coaxing, wheedling, flattery, cajolery, and, at times, criticism, from holding a short meeting to keeping the negotiators in continuous all-night session.

Social and political pressures include the opinion of outsiders whose views are important, and environmental influences. The parties to a dispute may be influenced by the views of other employers or trade unions, or of employers' organisations. Public opinion tends to be important in disputes affecting the supply of essential goods and services to the community. In certain situations, such as national emergencies, or when inflation is running wild, there is greater public concern over the way disputes are settled and wage claims dealt with. In a national emergency, in particular, the pressure to reach a settlement can lead to what is called non-stop bargaining or negotiations. The series of meetings, both joint and separate, may not only last the whole day but may continue through the following night and even longer. As a result the suggestion is sometimes made, perhaps not too seriously, that it is part of the conciliator's technique to use hunger, thirst and exhaustion to achieve his objectives.

Economic pressure relates to market conditions and the parties' bargaining strength. This is the pressure which the parties themselves seek to exert on each other. In negotiation or interest disputes, the economic forces at work are the primary factors which will influence a settlement. Pressure for a particular type of settlement will be generated by the factual situation— rise in living costs, wage increase granted by comparable firms, wage rates paid by competitors, comparable productivity levels, etc. As is also well known, economic pressure is more generally associated with the resort to a strike or lockout, a form of pressure which is of particular importance in countries where the parties are free to engage in industrial action before or during conciliation.

---

[1] Edgar L. Warren : "Mediation and fact finding", in A. Kornhauser, R. Dubin and A. M. Ross (eds.) : *Industrial conflict* (New York, McGraw-Hill, 1954), pp. 292-300.

As already indicated, it is the conciliator's task to exert pressure or to marshal and channel existing pressure in a way that will produce the most persuasive effect on the parties. The amount and kinds of pressure that will be necessary to induce a change in the parties' attitudes or position will depend on the circumstances. Probably in most cases the conciliator will need to employ a combination of personal and economic pressures.

The pressure that he will exert on the two parties will also vary. Because of the differences in their attitudes, he may need to exert more pressure on one party than on the other. At one stage of the negotiations he may need to continue exerting pressure on one party until it changes its position.

He will first rely on facts and reason. He may, if he thinks it will help, speak frankly and even critically to representatives who are clearly behaving in an unreasonable or obstructive manner. It must be stressed that this should be done only in separate meetings and when he has a good personal relationship with the party concerned. He must be certain that his standing is such that the representatives will accept critical comment without taking offence and without any feeling that he is biased. Clearly, the conciliator must be very sure of his ground before he ventures on such a positive line of action, and he should desist altogether if there is any doubt about the reaction he is likely to create.

In countries where the parties can declare a strike or lockout the parties' comparative bargaining strength is usually the most effective means of determining the pressures to be exerted on the two sides. Bargaining strength is not, however, only a question of the parties' financial resources or ability to shoulder the financial costs of a work stoppage. Full employment tends to strengthen the trade union, while large-scale unemployment has the opposite effect. Where skilled labour is in short supply, skilled workers and technicians occupy a strong bargaining position. Psychological factors may also be important in bolstering up the bargaining power of trade unions. Lack of a strike fund may not prevent a union from striking when it feels that its members are victims of great injustice. This may happen, for example, when workers are victimised for being trade unionists or when their wages are far below the prevailing rates. The workers may balance their willingness to withstand more suffering against the losses that they can inflict on the other side. The conciliator helps the parties in obtaining a full, realistic assessment of each other's bargaining strength.

Legislative restrictions on the right to strike or lockout and compulsory arbitration do not entirely eliminate the importance of economic pressures, but if such restrictions exist the marshalling of pressure will require the exercise of special skills on the part of the conciliator. The factual situation will still play a role and can be exploited by the conciliator to the fullest extent possible ; it will include the wage rates, fringe benefits and practices established by arbitration awards. Apart from this, the parties can be led to consider the advantages of an immediate voluntary settlement, as against the costs of prosecuting the dispute before the arbitration tribunal and the adverse effects of the ensuing delays on their relationship.

When the opportunity arises the conciliator may urge the parties to consider outside attitudes and opinions. He may seek the assistance of particularly influential outsiders to prevail upon one or the other party. Such outsiders will include the officials of employers' or trade union federations with which the parties are connected. In disputes of major importance the conciliator can point out to the parties how public opinion is developing. In developing countries he can point to the public concern for a state of labour relations which will facilitate economic development.

THE MANY SIDES OF THE CONCILIATOR

The question of conciliation techniques may also be considered from another angle—the fact that the conciliator is a multi-faceted individual, that his role comprises a variety of sub-roles, which are described in this section. The uses of these sub-roles can be more readily understood if one considers the main elements of the contribution that a conciliator makes in leading the parties to agreement. In directing his efforts towards this objective the conciliator is assisting the parties in a form of joint decision making. A conciliator's contribution may therefore be better understood by reference to the fact that decision making involves a choice among possible alternatives or options. From this point of view, a conciliator's contribution to the settlement of a dispute may be seen to consist of three basic categories of subsidiary contributions.

● The conciliator induces the parties to a course of action. His intervention in the dispute creates for the parties a situation different from the direct confrontation they had before. The conciliator establishes for the parties a need to re-examine their positions in this new situation and to consider possible alternatives or options. The need to make a choice of possible options continues after his initial intervention ; and, depending on the shifting pressures on the parties, he can sharpen or blur the need to make a choice.

● The conciliator opens to the parties a variety of available options besides those they can think of themselves. By probing into their attitudes and discovering in what fields they may be prepared to show some flexibility, he gains perspective of the issues in dispute and of alternative possibilities of settlement. These options may vary in number according to the nature of the issues involved ; and they may be available in respect of a single issue or a combination of issues. The conciliator controls the number of options to offer to the parties, and he may add to or reduce the number at any given time.

● The conciliator controls the timing for the selection of options. Just as the options may vary in number, their acceptability to the parties may vary from time to time. On the basis of his evaluation of the parties' attitudes and of the progress of the discussions, he can decide whether it is necessary to increase or shorten the time available for the selection of options ; his contribution is to offer the options at the opportune moment, when they are most likely to win a positive response from the parties.

A conciliator is able to make these contributions because he controls and guides the proceedings. It is again to be emphasised that he has only the power of reasoning and persuasion in moving the parties towards agreement. The following sections are devoted to a more detailed discussion of the conciliator's sub-roles. In exceptional cases it may suffice for the conciliator to rely only or chiefly on one or two sub-roles ; but in most cases he will be using more of them, in combination.

Discussion leader

As a discussion leader the conciliator reduces irrationality and antagonism between the parties. He guides them towards a problem-solving approach to their dispute ; he ensures that they discuss their differences in as friendly a manner as possible ; he helps them to analyse their problem, always striving to keep the analysis on rational ground ; he identifies the elements of the problem, both for the parties' benefit and for his own.

Alternative target or safety valve

The conciliator places himself in the position of alternative target when it is obvious to him that the parties are in an aggressive mood. Direct contact across the conference table will permit them to get it out of their system, but it involves the risk of lingering bitterness. The alternative is to set up a substitute target, one that will draw all the fire but from which none will be returned ; the parties can thus achieve an emotional release without direct and immediate damage to the negotiations. At other times the parties just have to express their feelings to someone, and have no one to turn to except the conciliator.

Communication link

There will be occasions when the disputants will not want to talk directly to each other, or when to bring them together in joint meetings will be fruitless or unnecessary. On these occasions the conciliator fulfils an important function as a communication link between the parties : serving as a communication link may either constitute his main conciliatory effort or be a contribution to it. But the conciliator is not simply a conduit through which information is passed or messages relayed from one side to the other ; he must be able to provide a thorough explanation, and to interpret the intentions of the parties.

Prober

There are few times during the negotiations that demand greater concentration from the conciliator than when he is trying to get the feel of where the disputants really stand and where they are heading. This is a probing effort to locate the unrevealed objectives, the stated claims that are mere façades, the real issues and the bargaining or "throw-away" items.

The conciliator will very seldom act in this capacity in a joint conference. He can expect to use separate meetings both to test the tentative reaction to a suggestion and to report on the reaction. He may send up such a trial balloon on his own initiative or at the instance of either party ; it is a means by which each side can assess the potential reaction of the other without officially shifting its own position. A successful probe can well be followed by major changes in position.

Source of information and ideas

For the parties in a dispute, often too deeply entrenched in their respective positions, the conciliator is an invaluable source of new information and new thoughts. In this sense he is also an innovator, particularly in providing the parties with different views of the issues, with possible alternative solutions and possibly an entirely new approach.

The conciliator may not go beyond offering the parties new ideas and insights, which will enable them to work out their own solutions, mainly between themselves. For example, the comparative data, of a more objective character, with which he is able to provide the parties may be all that they need to find a basis for settlement.

Sounding board

In a confidential capacity, the conciliator may use his information to indicate to the parties, outside each other's presence, which of their own arguments, defences and supports cannot stand under a rational, searching inquiry. Action that fits within this category is always limited to a separate or private meeting, and is never undertaken in a joint conference. It is appropriate for encouraging withdrawal or reduction of a demand.

Protector

In the process of direct bilateral negotiations the parties may be inhibited from exploring possible alternative solutions because of the fear of either party that it may thereby prematurely reveal the maximum concession it is prepared to make. This handicap is overcome in conciliation by the conciliator's role in protecting these parties' bargaining positions by exploring alternative solutions during separate meetings. It must be emphasised that this function is an essential aspect of the conciliator's confidential relationship with the parties. He can carry out such exploration only on the basis of confidential information they are willing to give him.

Fail-safe device

It is not unusual for a party to carry bluff too far or exaggerate its reaction to some move on the part of the other. Emotional stress, or the presence of onlookers, can lead negotiators to statements they soon regret. The conciliator can assist a party which has overstated its position or taken a clearly untenable stance to withdraw gracefully under the banner of reason.

Stimulator

Positive action is sometimes delayed because the push that will activate the group is lacking. Sensing this need, the conciliator can provide the necessary impulse ; he may make a concise statement, supply some data, give a hint or suggestion. Related to this is the function of the conciliator in crystallising changes of opinion as they occur. In the course of the discussion positive ideas may be advanced in nebulous form or referred to in a vague manner. At the appropriate moment he can intervene and give such ideas more definite form, expressing them in precise and concrete terms.

Sympathiser

There will be cases where the parties are very close to settlement, with full awareness that the last bit of flexibility is gone, and there is no readiness to make further concessions on either side. They may be persuaded to take the last small step that will close the gap, but either party will often wish to justify itself in doing so. In situations like this the conciliator is the sympathetic listener who will reassure them that the settlement they have worked out is probably satisfactory for their respective needs. Another time when the conciliator serves as a sympathetic listener is when the balance of strength is very one-sided and he has to satisfy the weaker party that it has probably obtained the best settlement it could under the circumstances.

Assessor or adviser

On request, the conciliator should provide an evaluation of matters relating to the negotiations. While it is generally desirable to wait for a request, he may volunteer to present his considered opinion if he feels that it will be helpful to the parties. A conciliator who is held in high esteem by the parties can unquestionably exert a powerful influence on the negotiations by the evaluations he is able to make.

Very often the settlement of a dispute is unnecessarily prolonged or the dispute develops into a very costly trial of strength because one party has misjudged the other's position, intentions and capabilities. The conciliator should see to it that such misinterpretations do not occur and that each side thoroughly understands the other's point of view, obtains a true picture of the opponent's strength and realises its own limitations and weaknesses. He should be able to tell one side when in his opinion a genuine last offer has been made by the other side or when the latter appears to have reached the limits of the concessions it is prepared to make.

While the making of evaluations is important, it is only one aspect of the advisory role of the conciliator. For the purposes of persuasion and exerting pressure the possibilities of the conciliator's advisory role are almost infinite. It is closely related to his role in serving as a source of new information, fresh ideas and alternative solutions. However, by giving advice, opinions or suggestions, the conciliator takes a more positive type of initiative : he actively espouses acceptance of a certain point of view ; he seeks to make a party take a decision in the way he has indicated. His advisory role especially requires of the conciliator the ability to put forward alternative solutions in such a way as to enable the parties to formulate them as their own instead of as those of the conciliator.

Advocate

The conciliation proceedings will eventually reach their final stages. The conciliator may either sense or be told outright that neither side intends to give any more ground, regardless of the consequences. When such a point is reached, the conciliator recognises the fact that the final moves have been made and he becomes an advocate for acceptance of the terms to which the parties have committed themselves at that stage, or of moves that will end the negotiations. He may forcefully argue or make an impassioned appeal for the acceptance of proposals that will settle the dispute, as a better alternative than a strike, a lockout or a settlement on terms dictated by an outsider.

He should make certain that both sides fully understand the consequences of their failure to arrive at an agreement.

Face-saver

In the situation just described the conciliator may eventually fulfil the role of a face-saver.[1] If the parties do not agree on the terms of a settlement, he may propose another agreed procedure for settling the dispute. Such a procedure, for example, may be the submission of the employer's last offer to acceptance or rejection by the union membership or the submission of the remaining unresolved issues to arbitration or, where highly technical questions are involved, to expert investigation and advice (fact finding).

Face-saving is a process in which the conciliator should normally be ready to assist, since it can often be a very important factor in keeping the peace. The need for it also arises either when a party knows from the outset or realises during the course of the proceedings that it has a weak case and can hope for little success in pursuing the dispute. The people concerned are often reluctant, however, to admit defeat, because they believe, rightly or wrongly, that this will involve them in a loss of face, or prestige, with their members and with the public. Face-saving can usually be accomplished by devising a form of words for announcing the settlement, which apparently makes some small concession to the party concerned but which in reality gives it little or nothing.

Coach or trainer

When the parties are relative newcomers to collective bargaining the conciliator can help them with respect to the procedural aspects of negotiation,

---

[1] The following example of the role of the conciliator in face-saving concerns a major dispute, in a situation in which each side appeared extremely mistrustful of the other. Identical terms of settlement were being proposed to labour and management, but each feared that if the other got wind of its willingness to settle, that attitude would be interpreted as a sign of weakness:

"(The conciliator) devised a special envelope system. It required each side to put one word, 'yes' or 'no', on a slip of paper in a plain sealed envelope. The envelopes were identical.

"That word was the answer to the question being asked simultaneously of management and of the union members : 'Do you accept the proposed terms of settlement ?'

"(The conciliator) sat in a hotel room, flanked by an observer from each side, and waited for an emissary from each side to bring him the one-word answer, sealed in the envelope. On receipt of the envelopes he shuffled them so no one would know which was which. Then, in the presence of the observers, he opened first one, then the other blank envelope. If he pulled the word 'no' out of each envelope, there would be no settlement.

"If he pulled 'yes' from one, and 'no' from the other, there would be no settlement. If he pulled 'yes' from each, the strike was over. What he drew were two 'yes' votes."

—"The mediators", reprinted from *Industrial Bulletin* (New York State Department of Labor), Feb. 1966.

especially on ways of improving their relations with an adversary. Where, for example, he knows that a party will reject a proposal by the other side, he may coach that party on how to formulate their rejection in diplomatic terms. This can be very helpful, since a blunt, outright rejection may only provoke indignation or aggravate antagonism on the part of the other party.

It has been suggested earlier that in developing countries, in cases where management and trade unions may as yet have little experience of collective bargaining, the process of conciliation can serve as a means of educating and training the parties with regard to the nature and conduct of bilateral negotiations. It has also been suggested that in such cases it would be useful for the conciliator, during his initial contacts with the parties, to brief them on the procedure of conciliation and its various aspects.

In any particular dispute the conciliator should not think that he has completed his job by giving such briefing, even if he repeats some of his points in his opening remarks at the first joint conference. It is actually in the course of the negotiations, as he guides the parties through their various stages, that he can give more practical and effective training by tendering the necessary hints, advice and explanations at every appropriate stage and on every suitable occasion.

It is not only with regard to parties relatively new to the collective bargaining process that the conciliator plays the role of a trainer. There may be a tendency on the part of parties with already substantial experience of negotiations to lean too heavily on the conciliator. They may adopt the attitude that they have done all they can do towards reaching a settlement and that it is now up to the conciliator to find the solution. In short, they try to place the responsibility entirely on him. This attitude should be firmly resisted, and the parties told plainly that it is their dispute and that it is for them to arrive at an agreement. While the conciliator's function is to assist them in every possible way, they are not thereby relieved of their responsibility. Only the parties themselves can provide the means of solving their problem; they must never be allowed to think that the conciliator has a magic wand which will produce the answer out of a hat, as they will do all too readily if they are allowed to shift the responsibility onto him. It is only on the basis of their contributions that he can work.

PROPOSALS AND COUNTER-PROPOSALS

By the parties

During separate meetings tentative proposals for a settlement are often put forward rather vaguely by the negotiators. The conciliator can seize this opportunity of probing their intentions and produce a written statement defining as clearly as possible what they have in mind. When they have agreed that the written formula which he has produced accurately records their proposals, he can take it to the other side. The latter will, at first sight, almost certainly reject it out of hand, but may after further examination suggest alterations in the wording which will make it acceptable to them. The amended version will then be taken back to its originators, who may either accept the suggested amendments or propose further changes.

This process of carrying a written formula back and forth between the two sides can go on for quite some time and provide a test for the conciliator's patience, but it can promote an effective exchange of views, leading to a settlement. Moreover it has the advantage of ensuring that the tentative terms of an agreement are already expressed in writing at a early stage. The formula ultimately agreed upon after successive amendments may bear very little resemblance to the original proposal, but that is of little consequence ; it is useful to start with something in writing on which the two sides can focus their attention. This approach, of course, is not appropriate when the dispute centres entirely on the amount of an increase in wages, because that is simply a question of how much, and does not call for extensive drafting. When conditions are attached to a wage increase, however, it is useful to state them in writing, unless they are beyond dispute.

One device which a conciliator may find useful in certain circumstances is not to reveal immediately to the other side the first concessions which are made by one of the parties and which the latter authorises him to convey to the other side. Disclosing them at an early stage may have the effect of encouraging the other side to stand firm, in the hope of extracting further concessions. If, however, a situation can be brought about in which the conciliator has concessions from both sides and neither side is aware of the fact, he is in a position to measure the gap between them and assess what has to be done to close it. In some cases the proposals of one side may match or, very exceptionally, even exceed the requirements of the other, and in those circumstances the conciliator's task in arranging the final settlement becomes a relatively easy one.

Another device to which the conciliator may resort is to co-ordinate or synchronise the making of mutual concessions by the two sides at joint meetings. The conciliator may ask each side during separate meetings not to put forward any proposal or counter-proposal at a joint meeting without first discussing and clearing it with him. In particular he may advise one side against advancing a proposal representing the maximum concession it will be prepared to make ; such advice is appropriate if the other side is still far from being in a reasonable bargaining position, and may not be willing to take the same, long, forward step as the former.

By the conciliator

In the view of many people the compromise sought for in conciliation is largely a matter of "splitting the difference". This would make the job of the conciliator a very easy one, but nothing can be further from the truth. Let us say, for example, that a union's proposal is for a wage increase of 90 cents a day. The company replies that in view of competitive conditions it cannot afford an increase of more than 20 cents. After some discussions, the union lowers its demand to 70 cents and the company increases its offer to 30 cents. At this point, each side maintains that it is not prepared to make any further concession. There is therefore a difference of 40 cents between the parties' positions. Should the conciliator propose, on the principle of splitting the difference, a wage increase of 50 cents (30 + 20)? If he does so, he will most certainly meet a resounding rebuff from the company. In practice, that is not the way conciliators work towards a compromise.

In the situation just described the parties' positions are still too far apart and do not provide a realistic basis for the conciliator to make a proposal for settlement. He has still some hard work to do to persuade either or both of the parties to make a further movement towards a more reasonable bargaining position. He assesses the reasonableness of the parties' positions on the basis of the information he has obtained regarding the issues involved—comparative wage data, relevant practices, productivity levels, etc., among other employers. It follows that his ability to discharge this responsibility depends on the amount of preparation he has made; and he can persuade more effectively if he can make use of fuller information than the parties themselves possess.

In the example above the situation will be different if the conciliator is able to reduce the difference between the two sides to a point where the union's demand is, for example, 46 cents and the company's offer 44 cents. A conciliator's proposal in this situation can be 44 cents or 46 cents or any amount between them : it does not have to be necessarily 45 cents but it may be so ; in view of all the relevant factors, it may also be 44.5 cents, or 45.5 cents, and so on. The important thing is that the conciliator should have facts and arguments to back up his proposal. The parties must be able to see that it is a valid and wise proposal.

On wage issues the conciliator's proposal may cover both the amount of wage increase and the way it is to be applied. When there is still disagreement over the amount of the increase, the difficulty may be overcome by a proposal regarding its application. Where, for example, the proposed duration of the collective agreement being negotiated is two years, the compromise may be for half of the increase to be paid immediately and the balance after one year. In many developing countries it seems usual to nego-tiate collective agreements for a duration of one year. In this situation an employer may not agree to a proposed increase which he will have to pay immediately; he may, however, agree to the increase on condition that he will pay only half of it the first year and the balance afterwards. This means that the conciliator will also have to propose that the duration of the collective agreement be extended to two years. The provision of a longer term for the collective agreement may in fact be beneficial to the development of the parties' relationship.

SITUATIONS ADMITTING
OF LITTLE COMPROMISE

10

The discussion in the preceding two chapters has been largely concerned with the resolution of issues which leave sufficient room for compromise, i.e. demands for wage increases, improved fringe benefits or other improvements in conditions of employment, as well as arrangements concerning relations between the parties, including trade union security, collective bargaining and joint consultation procedures ; these are essentially issues in respect of which a settlement can be achieved on the basis of mutual concessions. As shown in Chapter 2, issues of that kind are more particularly involved in interest disputes. In the other types of disputes the issues do not readily lend themselves to compromise solutions. The present chapter covers other or additional approaches available to a conciliator dealing with disputes of the latter kind ; it also covers the handling of strike and lockout situations, which presuppose some reluctance to compromise.

DISPUTES OVER TRADE UNION RIGHTS AND WORKERS' GRIEVANCES

The disputes with which we are here concerned are disputes arising from acts of anti-union discrimination, i.e. unfair labour practices ; disputes over the recognition of trade unions for collective bargaining purposes ; and disputes over workers' grievances.

One preliminary point may be noted. These disputes frequently arise from a past occurrence. In any particular dispute the issue involved may be essentially a question of fact. Issues of fact are invariably involved in unfair labour practice disputes and in many forms of workers' grievances : one side bases its stand on its version of the facts while the other side has its totally different or opposite version.

An issue of fact is not a matter for compromise. All that the conciliator can do is to help the parties in ascertaining the real facts. For this purpose a conciliation meeting becomes a sort of hearing where the parties present their evidence. Obviously the conciliator should not try to invest the proceedings with the formal atmosphere of a judicial trial.

In dealing with issues of fact the conciliator functions very much in the same capacity as an arbitrator or judge. He has only the evidence presented by the parties to guide him, and he informs them of his findings of fact. There is, of course, an important difference; unlike an arbitrator or judge the conciliator does not issue an award or decision; he can only suggest or propose a settlement in accordance with his findings. And, as in the case of interest disputes, he may have to make use of all his powers of persuasion to induce the parties to accept both his findings and his recommendation.

Unfair labour practices

In a typical dispute concerning an alleged unfair labour practice a worker is dismissed for serious misconduct and the worker or his union contests the employer's decision, claiming that the dismissal is really trade union victimisation. If the conciliator's findings support the employer's contention, i.e. that the dismissal was in fact due to the worker's misconduct, the conciliator's recommendation may be the end of the matter. If, however, the facts show the contrary, i.e. that the worker was really a victim of anti-union discrimination, the process of settling the dispute becomes an extremely difficult task.

Since an unfair labour practice is invariably due to the employer's dislike of trade unions or his opposition to the presence of a trade union in his plant, the task of the conciliator is essentially one of persuasion to bring about a fundamental change in the employer's attitude. This is a very delicate matter, because he will be questioning what the employer may consider to be a vital question of principle. The employer may believe that it is his fundamental right to run his business as he likes without interference on the part of other people, including members of a trade union. The conciliator will therefore need to act in the most prudent and tactful way to enlighten the employer about trade unionism in modern society.

The existence in certain countries of legislative provisions penalising unfair labour practices as criminal offences does not usually prevent trade unions from raising disputes over the commission of such acts, since the main concern of the unions is to obtain the reinstatement of dismissed workers, a remedy not normally available in criminal proceedings. However, such provisions may be useful in persuading the employer to effect an amicable settlement.

The conciliator may feel that his individual efforts will be futile or of little avail. Accordingly if the employer belongs to an employers' association the conciliator may call for assistance on an official or influential member of the association who may be able to persuade the employer. In addition, or in other cases, the conciliator may seek the assistance of other influential persons in employers' circles who have had fairly satisfactory relations with trade unions or who hold progressive views on the subject.

Recognition disputes

A typical recognition dispute arises when an employer denies a request by a trade union that it be recognised by the employer as the collective bargaining representative of the category of his employees specified in the request. The request may be made with a view to the conclusion of a recognition agreement or as one of several items proposed by the union for negotiating a collective agreement relating to terms of employment.

The conciliator's approach will depend on the employer's motive for refusing recognition. If it was due to a general antagonism to trade unions or prejudice against them, the conciliator will have to perform essentially the same task of enlightenment and persuasion as in the case of an unfair labour practice. In this case too he may request the assistance of leading members of the employers' organisation concerned, and of progressive-minded employers, to use their influence in persuading the employer to change his attitude.

The conciliator faces a different problem if the employer does not have a negative attitude towards trade unions in general but does not want to recognise a particular union because he does not consider it to be sufficiently representative of the workers concerned. In that case the conciliator may try to persuade the employer to accord recognition on the basis of certain agreed criteria, such as the union's membership strength, or support on the part of the workers concerned. The same technique can be employed where the dispute has arisen over the conflicting claims of two or more rival unions to represent the same group of workers.

In certain countries, in the absence of legislation, criteria for determining the question of trade union recognition have been developed in practice, or laid down in voluntary codes of principles or industrial relations charters agreed to by employers' and workers' organisations and sometimes also by the government. The existence of such agreed criteria will be of great use to conciliators ; and if there are relevant provisions in voluntary codes of principles or industrial relations charters, he can also invoke the aid of the employers' and workers' organisations that have accepted them.

The membership strength of a trade union can be difficult to determine. The union may state a membership figure which the employer does not accept. The employer may then demand that the names of the trade union members be supplied to him, but the union may be afraid to supply them for fear of victimisation. The conciliator can avoid this kind of deadlock by suggesting that the records of both the employer and the trade union should be opened for inspection by an independent accountant, who will give a certificate of the proportion of union members employed. This process of verification may also be carried out by the conciliation service itself, through an arrangement under which the employer sends in a list of all his employees in the category in question, and the union similarly supplies a list of all its members employed in that category by the employer. A conciliation officer then compares the two lists, records the names that are in both lists, and calculates from this the proportion of union members in the total employed. He then provides a certificate stating that proportion to the employer and the union, without giving any indication of the names of trade union members.

Grievance disputes

The categories of grievance disputes that will come before conciliators in different countries will vary according to national practice. In its most common form a grievance dispute will have originated in a protest by a worker against some act or decision of the management. As was stated in Chapter 2, the scope for compromise in grievance disputes is restricted in as far as there is some identifiable standard for settlement—a statutory provision, employment contract, collective agreement, arbitration award or works rule, or the custom or usage on which the grievance was based. In countries where grievance disputes may ultimately be submitted to labour courts for adjudication, standards for their settlement are built up through the rulings laid down by the court decisions, which eventually form a body of case law or industrial jurisprudence for the guidance of employers and trade unions. A distinction needs to be made between different categories of grievance disputes.

(a) "Yes or no" cases

A grievance dispute may involve a single issue requiring a simple "yes" or "no" answer : Was the employer justified in taking the action or decision that gave rise to the grievance ? If from the facts the answer is "no", and if the employer is found to have violated, for example, a provision of a collective agreement, the conciliator will normally have no alternative but to recommend a settlement in accordance with the terms of the agreement.

While the task of the conciliator in ascertaining the facts may be relatively easy, it may not be as easy for him to persuade the losing party to accept his findings and recommendation for settlement. Because of the great variety of grievance disputes and the infinite variety of the circumstances that can give rise to workers' grievances, it is not possible to suggest specifically what a conciliator may do when the losing party tells him that it cannot accept his findings or recommendation.

Possibly, in clear-cut cases, he may resort to the device referred to earlier of seeking the assistance of the officials of employers' organisations or of workers' organisations at a higher level in order to persuade the employer or trade union involved in the dispute. He can undoubtedly be more persuasive and effective if he can back up his recommendations with facts and practical examples drawn from the experience of other firms; for that purpose he can always seek to increase his knowledge of labour relations problems and practices inside undertakings.

(b) Disciplinary action

A large proportion of grievance disputes arise from disciplinary action taken by employers for alleged misconduct on the part of the workers. The misconduct may range from a crime, such as theft or assault on a supervisor, to comparatively minor breaches of conditions of employment such as lateness.

Disciplinary disputes set difficult problems when they come before a conciliator. They can be fraught with bitterness and hostility when the penalty imposed was dismissal. They can lead to strikes when fellow workers take sympathetic action in support of those who have incurred penalties. On the other hand, some employers still adhere to the conception that the "right to hire or fire" is a management prerogative, which they resent having to discuss with trade union officials. The prestige of supervisors and managers is also frequently involved. Nevertheless, it is often possible for a conciliator to establish the facts and by so doing to convince either the employer that he acted without just cause or was too severe, or the union that the penalty was well deserved.

(c) Application and interpretation of collective agreements

The conciliator faces a different problem in dealing with grievance disputes arising from collective agreements when the disputes do not fall into the category of "yes or no" cases discussed above. Grievances may arise because of ambiguity or the very general character of the language of a collective agreement. In the case of a comprehensive agreement, there may be doubts about the application of a particular clause to a given situation. Not infrequently, questions arise with regard to issues that are not covered by any specific provision of the agreement. In these cases the main issue will be one of interpretation : What was the intention of the parties?

The problem of the conciliator in dealing with such a case may be made clearer by comparing his role with that of a judge in a labour court in a similar case. The judge conducts a hearing, takes the evidence submitted by the parties and may make such further inquiries as he thinks necessary. He then weighs all the evidence and information he has obtained, determines the facts essential to the resolution of the issue and makes his decision on the basis of his findings.

The conciliator makes a similar effort to find out what are the facts of the case. But unlike a judge in a labour court, he does not sit down to write a decision stating how the issue should be resolved. One course that he may follow is to discuss with each party what he considers to be a good solution. If one party refuses it, the conciliator can put forward an alternative to be discussed in the same way. This process can go on until a solution is found that is acceptable to both parties. There are, of course, other ways in which he can test the parties' reactions to various possible solutions.

The agreed solution may be a simple clarification of the provision of the collective agreement in question; on the other hand it may amount to a modification or even a substantial amendment of that provision, or it may involve the introduction of an entirely new one. What is important is that the parties should have considered different possible ways of solving their problem and should have agreed upon one which they consider the best, probably not only as a solution to the problem of the moment but also for their future relations. It must be stressed that the conciliator will assist the parties in weighing the advantages and disadvantages of each proposed solution.

(d) Law enforcement and conciliation

The conciliation of grievance disputes arising from the application of legislative provisions is closely related to the problem of the enforcement of labour law. In dealing with a grievance dispute in this category a conciliator is not acting as a labour inspector or labour law officer; in his capacity as a conciliator he should not intervene in a case which is clearly one for law enforcement. In practice, however, there will be cases in which it will be difficult to determine whether the problem calls for law enforcement or for conciliation. The answer may have to be found in the definition of the respective responsibilities of the labour inspectorate and the conciliation service, in administrative rules for dealing with such borderline or doubtful cases and in the arrangements for co-operation between the two services.

Even where only law enforcement is involved, however, there will be occasions when some form of intervention by conciliators may be useful. For example, an employer may have flagrantly broken the law, and thus considerably angered the workers, and the union may wish to retaliate by a demonstration and a strike. Or an employer may have committed over some length of time a series of breaches of labour law, and resentment on the part of the workers may have been building up and be on the point of exploding into mass action. In either case there is a situation involving elements of labour conflict, where the supposed victims of the breach of the law are by-passing the labour inspection service ; the tactful approach of a conciliator can be of great help in calming people down and in persuading the workers to make use of available legal remedies instead of resorting to direct action.

(e) Grievances and contract negotiations

A conciliator will have no special procedural problem in dealing with a grievance dispute on its own. However, in lists of demands or proposals that they present to employers, trade unions in various developing countries not infrequently include not only claims relating to wages and other terms of employment but also demands for the redress of specific workers' grievances.

It does not follow that in every case involving these two sets of issues (conflicts of interest and grievances), the conciliator should always proceed with the conciliation of the dispute as a whole. The time needed to dispose of the grievance issues can considerably delay the negotiations over the conflict of interests, since it will be necessary to hear the workers concerned, their supervisors and other witnesses whom the parties may present. Such delays can be serious complicating factors in cases in which strike notices have been issued, in which there is a strike deadline, or in which the legislation prescribes a period during which the conciliation proceedings should be concluded. In addition, when the union considers the grievances to be of particular importance (as in a case in which the dismissal of workers is claimed to constitute victimisation or to have been wholly unjustified), the grievances can create a sour atmosphere for the discussion of the economic issues.

Accordingly the conciliator should not feel bound to deal simultaneously with the two sets of issues involved in the dispute ; he may also consider going ahead with only one set of issues and arranging for the other to be dealt with in later or separate proceedings. Before he makes up his mind, the conciliator should sound the union's attitude in regard to the various grievances. His soundings may reveal that some of them have been included in the union's demands as throw-away items, for the purpose mainly of giving moral satisfaction to the workers concerned. Among the grievances the redress of which the union intends seriously to pursue, a sounding of both sides may also reveal that a number can be easily disposed of ; the employer, like the union, may show a positive, conciliatory attitude. In such cases, the satisfactory settlement of these grievances at an early stage of the negotiations may in fact facilitate the discussion of the economic issues.

On the other hand it may be necessary for the conciliator to arrange separate proceedings to deal with grievances that will require extended hearings, particularly grievances with heavy emotional overtones. In most cases the union will probably agree to have the grievances dealt with later, but there may be occasions where it will want them to be given prior consideration. Another possibility will be open to the conciliator in countries where grievance disputes may be referred by the government or on application by one party to a labour court; if it is important that the grievances be settled as early as possible and if there is no other conciliator to whom they can be transferred, he may propose this possibility. Depending on national practice, the conciliator can also suggest that the parties should submit the grievances to an arbitrator of their own choice.

STRIKE AND LOCKOUT SITUATIONS

In dealing with a strike or lockout situation a conciliator will necessarily be guided by the law of his country and any administrative instructions or directives on the matter. Subject to this, his problem is to decide on a course of action that will facilitate the orderly conduct of the dispute and its settlement.

On-going strikes and lockouts

We have seen earlier that where a dispute arises from a breakdown in the negotiations for a collective agreement, the occurrence of a strike or lockout will affect the timing of the intervention of a conciliator in the dispute, or at least of the first joint conference to be arranged by him. Until the parties have agreed to resume negotiations under his guidance the conciliator can do much to keep open the lines of communication between them. He may frequently check with the representatives of the parties with a view to arranging a joint meeting as early as possible.

When negotiations have been resumed he can try to arrange a return-to-work agreement pending resolution of the issues in dispute. Quite often this will turn out to be a case of conciliation within conciliation, since it involves agreeing on the conditions under which work will be resumed. In the case of a strike, for example, the union may raise the question of the date from which any wage increase that may be finally agreed upon shall be payable, or it may request a temporary concession pending final settlement of the dispute.

When there is only a threat or notice of strike, the strike deadline brings pressure to bear on the parties and stimulates them to serious bargaining. The actual beginning of a strike removes this pressure, and it then becomes the task of the conciliator to create other pressures, or bring other pressures to bear on the parties. He may use personal pressure, and indicate that he will withdraw for a time if no progress is made in the negotiations. This technique will be useful if one or both of the negotiating committees may not want to confront the people they represent with the fact that the conciliator has temporarily withdrawn with a "no progress" announcement. A conciliator should be alert to the use that can be made of the pressures of economic factors, or of public opinion and public concern over the continuation of the work stoppage. [1]

A conciliator faces another type of situation where he has to deal with an unofficial or wildcat strike, i.e. one that takes place without the official authorisation or support of the trade union concerned. They occur frequently over grievance issues, and sometimes they are spontaneous protests by a group of workers against a management decision.

As a matter of broad principle, in cases of wildcat strikes, a conciliator should not respond to a request for his intervention from unofficial strike leaders. To do so would not only antagonise the employer concerned but would also diminish trade union discipline and the authority and status of trade union officials. This does not mean that he is precluded from taking action, but he should approach the responsible trade union officials with a view to their taking the necessary steps to persuade the workers to return to work and prosecute their claims through the established or agreed procedures.

Threatened strikes and lockouts

In countries where strikes and lockouts can lawfully be declared before or during conciliation, situations in which conciliators are faced with actual work stoppages at the time of their intervention are not frequent, and may be very rare. More often they have to deal with situations in which a strike or lockout is threatened.

The fact that such a threat exists or a strike or lockout notice has been given in a dispute should not affect the attitude of impartiality of the conciliator in regard to the party concerned, although one aspect of his role in such a situation is to advise the parties on the observance of any legal requirements (such as a period of notice or the taking of a strike ballot) for staging a strike or lockout. The regulations may require him to assist in organising and conducting a strike ballot.

The conciliator will of course be expected to hold meetings with the two sides, but will probably find that if the commencing date of the strike or lockout is still some time ahead, there is little readiness on their part to make any moves ; as the strike or lockout deadline draws nearer the pressures upon

---

[1] See Simkin, op. cit., pp. 93-94.

them intensify and more realistic attitudes begin to develop. Even so, it may take a series of meetings spread over days or weeks before any real progress is made. The negotiations may continue until just shortly before the strike or lockout is scheduled to begin. It is to some extent inevitable that each side will tend to wait until the last moment to see whether the other side's resolve will break first, and as a result the negotiations will tend to be conducted in a tense and dramatic atmosphere.

One of the questions that a conciliator will often ask himself is whether he should request the postponement of a proposed strike. The effect of a postponement, however, is to remove the immediate pressure of an approaching strike deadline. If, therefore, a proposal for postponement is to be made—

...the timing is important. If it is made too early, it will tend to destroy the usefulness of deadline pressures. If the parties know that a request for postponement will be made and that both are likely to agree to it, they may seize upon this as an excuse for avoiding the difficult last-minute decisions that precede a real strike or lockout threat. Conversely, if it is made too late, the strike or lockout procedures may be so far advanced that it is almost impossible to reverse them.

These considerations are complicated further by the fact that any actual contract extension or postponement brings up new questions. What about retroactive pay? How long an extension is appropriate? Should an extension preserve all or only some of the provisions of the expiring contract? Will the company attempt to continue operations if a strike does occur? These and other questions, injected into negotiations in the most critical hours or minutes, could block a settlement. [1]

It will be seen that making a request for extension of the strike deadline, which may seem to an outsider to be a simple and sensible tactical move on the part of the conciliator, in fact calls for consideration of very complicated questions—besides which the result of such an extension is sometimes doubtful. If the main problem is lack of time for agreement and there is some real hope of achieving a settlement by extending the deadline, a request made at the right moment may be advisable ; but if positions have so hardened that additional time is not likely to make any difference, there is no point in delaying what may be inevitable. If the conciliator concludes that postponement is advisable, he should make sure that both parties will accept his request. If it is rejected, the fact that it was made will have muddled the negotiations, and may even have helped to precipitate a strike. [2]

Finally, if a work stoppage is inevitable, the conciliator can help the parties to agree on arrangements for the orderly shut-down of operations and for the maintenance of essential safety services while the strike is in progress. The purpose of such arrangements is to ensure the immediate resumption of production once the dispute has been settled.

---

[1] Simkin, op. cit., p. 87.
[2] Ibid., pp. 87-88.

If industrial action is to take place, the negotiations will usually have been broken off before the deadline. It may happen, however, that the negotiations before the conciliator are still going on when the deadline is reached. If the parties are not so far apart and the atmosphere seems favourable, the conciliator may make an effort to persuade the parties not to interrupt their negotiations. Obviously he should not insist on such a course of action if he senses from the feelings of the parties that nothing can be gained from it. It is possible that once the strike or lockout stage has been reached, to bring the representatives of the parties together immediately will only expose them to mutual irritation. The conciliator may then deal with the situation as in the case of an on-going work stoppage discussed above.

CONCLUSION OF CONCILIATION PROCEEDINGS, AND SUBSEQUENT ACTION

11

When a conciliator's efforts to settle a dispute come to an end he must take certain action to wind up his handling of the case. In particular, he will participate, to a varying extent, in the drafting of any agreement reached ; he will write a final report on his intervention ; and he will assist the parties, and in some cases the authorities, in initiating further proceedings if his conciliation has not been fully successful.

DRAFTING OF AGREEMENT, IF ANY

If a dispute is settled, the fact will be reflected in an agreement. A conciliator usually adds his signature to an agreement reached during conciliation proceedings, but the asistance he may provide in the drafting of the agreement is a matter of national practice. He may play an active part in the drafting, or the parties may do the drafting by themselves, presenting the final text to him to see if it correctly embodies all that had been agreed upon. In the latter case if he has any material change to suggest he should do so on the basis of a written record he has made during the discussions with regard to the issue in question.

For parties newly initiated into collective bargaining, advice by the conciliator on how the agreement should be drafted can undoubtedly be very helpful. He should therefore be prepared, unless he is for some reason precluded from doing so, to respond affirmatively if they should request him to help them with the drafting.

In the course of the negotiations the parties may reach agreement on an issue without formulating the precise terms in which the clause relating to it should be drafted. In these cases the conciliator can provide the parties with model clauses drawn from other collective agreements which have proved satisfactory in practice.

With regard to the form of written conciliation settlement, practice differs from one country to another. In essence, however, an agreement reached by conciliation is no different from one reached through unassisted collective bargaining. There is a certain psychological value in having conciliation agreements drafted in the same way as ordinary collective agreements : it emphasises the fact that the agreement was made by the parties themselves and on their own responsibility. This understanding can be a favourable factor in the negotiations for the renewal of the agreement—as a collective agreement. Therefore where he is free to do so, a conciliator should consider the advisability of suggesting to the parties that the agreement they have reached should be drafted in the form of a collective agreement.

FAILURE TO REACH AGREEMENT

Any necessary formalities for bringing conciliation proceedings to a close will be largely a matter of national practice, depending on local laws and regulations. Under the law of certain countries, some formalities may be required in connection with provisions limiting the duration of conciliation proceedings or prohibiting strikes and lockouts while conciliation proceedings are pending, and sometimes also during a prescribed period after they have been concluded. However, the question is of practical importance only when conciliation has failed to bring about a settlement relating to the substance of a dispute.

In countries where there is no limitation on the duration of conciliation proceedings and where the parties are free to stage strikes or lockouts a conciliator will persist in his appointed duty as long as neither party has broken off the negotiations. It is indeed difficult for a conciliator to accept defeat ; but if prolonged discussions have been held in a case without any perceptible result, a point may be reached at which he has to admit that further efforts on his part will be fruitless. In such a case he may frankly give the parties his assessment of the situation, and inform them that he is not calling any further meeting but that he will be available at the request of either party in the event of any new development. This is not an agreeable task, and the conciliator has to carry it out in a most tactful manner, without giving any hint of blame on either party for the failure of the current negotiations.

In practice, a conciliator is spared from taking such course of action by the arrival of the strike deadline and the consequent breaking-off of the negotiations. However, the intervention of the conciliator in such a case does not necessarily come to an end, since it is still his job to bring about a resumption of the negotiations.

CONCILIATION REPORTS

In some countries it is left to the government's discretion, if conciliation fails, to refer a dispute to another procedure of settlement. The administrative guidelines for conciliators that will have been laid down to cover that possibility may require a recommendation by a conciliator in his final report on the matter.

There seems to be a great deal of difference from country to country with regard to the preparation of reports by conciliators on cases handled by them. The differences may relate not only to form and content but also to the number of reports to be submitted in respect of each case. These differences in turn are likely to be due to differences in the importance attached to conciliation and in the purposes for which reports are required. In some countries a conciliator may have to prepare only a final report for each case. In others he may have to send in also an initial report, and even a report on every conciliation meeting convened by him.

A conciliator will therefore submit reports in accordance with the practice of his country. In principle, conciliators should not be required to go into so much detail as to make the preparation of reports excessively time-consuming. The work can be greatly facilitated if reports can be prepared on printed forms, with blank spaces to be filled in or boxes to be checked or crossed, and enough space for remarks where the conciliator can relate such details as he feels desirable.

Whatever the national practice, a conciliator should give due attention to the preparation of his reports. He should try to discover the purposes which such reports are supposed to serve in his country, so that he can prepare his reports accordingly. He should also bear in mind that since he is not directly supervised by his superiors while discharging his duties, his reports provide a basis on which they can form an opinion of his competence and efficiency.

One of the purposes of preparing initial reports may be to inform the headquarters office or the conciliator's superior officers of the existence of disputes as they occur. The provision of this information is especially necessary with regard to disputes which have more than local effects and repercussions, or in respect of which work stoppages are threatened or have occurred. From the early reports sent in by a conciliator, the headquarters office may see whether he should be sent any information, or any advice regarding further action.

Needless to say, conciliation reports are important sources of information for policy making and the study of remedial measures in the field of industrial relations. Conciliators are in the best position to gather information on the causes of industrial disputes and generally information with a bearing on the problems of industrial peace.

Once a conciliator has finished dealing with a dispute, his reports on it become part of the history of the relations between the parties. The information contained in this part of the case history on file may be useful for conciliation in a future dispute between the same parties.

The final report will show the results of the conciliator's intervention : the issues on which agreement, if any, has been reached, and the issues which remain unresolved. The conciliator may make recommendations regarding further action. There is, however, probably one thing he should avoid, namely to try to assess the responsibility of either party—or blame them—for failure to reach agreement. There is no useful purpose to be served by putting such an assessment in writing. Even if the document is confidential, there is a danger that its contents may come to the knowledge of the party concerned, and that the conciliator may incur resentment and thereby lose his usefulness as a future conciliator vis-à-vis that party. On the other hand he should not feel precluded from expressing his personal views to other conciliators who may request information on the persons he has had dealings with.

SUBSEQUENT ACTION

It is sometimes too readily assumed that there are only two possible outcomes of conciliation, either success in reaching a settlement of the dispute or failure, probably resulting in a work stoppage, or continuance of a stoppage if one has already begun. Ideally, of course, it is the objective of the conciliator to close the gap between the two sides so that they are able to reach complete agreement, but the fact has to be faced that there are occasions when this is not possible. A conciliator is still performing an extremely useful function, even when he fails to bring about a settlement, if he can nevertheless persuade the parties to attempt to settle the dispute by peaceful means and without resorting to some form of industrial action. Such attempts may be made through informal procedures developed by administrative practice as well as through more formal procedures provided for by legislation.

Informal procedures

If a dispute has not been settled in substance by conciliation, the parties may accept a proposal by the conciliator for settling the dispute through an agreed informal procedure, under which the conciliator may be called upon to take further action.

(a) Workers' ballot

For example, the negotiators may agree to submit the employer's last offer to a vote by the workers, on the understanding that if a majority of the workers vote to accept the offer the dispute shall be settled on those terms. It may be desirable in such a case to establish safeguards to ensure that the terms of the offer are fairly presented to the workers by the management and trade union negotiators. The conciliator may assist in establishing such safeguards and, also, if desired by the parties, in conducting the ballot.

(b) Reference to a senior conciliator

Among the informal procedures is a further attempt at conciliation by a senior conciliation officer or a senior official of the conciliation service. This device may prove effective in a case in which the original conciliator has succeeded in obtaining agreement on all but one or two of the issues in dispute. If the remaining unresolved issues are of a technical character, the renewed attempt at conciliation may be entrusted to a labour relations specialist. There is, however, a danger that too frequent resort to this device may reduce the effectiveness of the conciliators who deal with disputes in the first place. Moreover, when it is resorted to, it should be made clear that no reflection is intended to be cast on the competence of the original conciliator.

Another informal procedure involves action by the head of the national conciliation service or the regional office to which the original conciliator belongs. This device is based on the fact that when a conciliator makes a proposal to the parties for a settlement he usually does so not by a written recommendation but orally in a meeting with them. The value of a formal recommendation embodying proposals for settling a dispute lies in the moral authority of its author. In certain cases it may be advantageous to use this formula when a conciliator fails to settle a dispute ; in order to give added moral authority to the written recommendation it should be made by the head of the conciliation service or the regional office concerned. The recommendation will take account of the final report of the original conciliator, but it should also be made after consultations with him and should not be a mere repetition of a proposal he may himself have made to the parties.

Formal procedures

With regard to the more formal settlement procedures that may be followed if a conciliator fails to settle a dispute, the most common is reference to a conciliation board, to a fact-finding body or to arbitration. In some countries only one of these possibilities may be available ; in others there may be a choice. Arbitration leads to a final settlement of the dispute by the award or decision of the arbitration tribunal. Under the conciliation board or fact-finding procedures, the settlement depends on the parties' agreement.

(a) Conciliation boards

Practices regarding the composition and functioning of conciliation boards have been mentioned in Chapter 1. In general, when a board is constituted on an ad hoc basis, its terms of reference will be set forth in the instrument by which it is appointed. It is usually given powers of investigation not generally enjoyed by an individual conciliator, including the power to require the production of documents. The procedure of a conciliation board also differs from that of an individual conciliator in another respect : a board is usually required to make recommendations on how a dispute should be settled. In practice, however, the need for making formal written recommendations may arise only if the board does not succeed in persuading the parties to reach agreement through discussion.

(b) Fact finding

The fact-finding procedure is generally applied to disputes of some importance, often as a method of emergency adjustment when compulsory arbitration is not available. It is usually entrusted to an hoc body called a court or board of inquiry, but in some countries is undertaken by permanent labour relations bodies. The authority empowered to appoint a board or court of inquiry is also usually authorised to fix the number of its members. In some countries they are independent and neutral persons only, in others they include employer and worker members. In some countries fact finding is also resorted to in disputes of less importance, and is carried out by a less formal kind of body, usually a committee of investigation, which may consist of one member only.

The main function of a board or court of inquiry is to investigate the facts and circumstances of the dispute or matter referred to it, and its terms of reference will be defined in the instrument by which it is constituted. It may be set up exclusively as a fact-finding body. It conducts its proceedings in a relatively formal manner, keeping a record of the statements and evidence presented by the parties.

The report of the fact-finding body is submitted to the government. In some countries the report is to be laid before the legislature. However, the essential characteristics of the fact-finding procedure is the publication of the report. It is expected that public opinion will be formed on the basis of the facts brought out in the report, and this expectation will exert some pressure upon the parties towards a settlement of the dispute.

If a fact-finding body is empowered to make recommendations, it will be functioning in essentially the same way as a conciliation board, although there may be differences in the manner in which the two bodies perform their functions. A dispute will be wholly resolved if the parties accept the recommendations of a conciliation board or fact-finding body. Otherwise, the recommendations provide a basis for further negotiations between the parties and further conciliation efforts.

(c) Voluntary arbitration

If a dispute is submitted to voluntary arbitration the assistance of the conciliator may be useful, or requested by the parties, for drawing up the arbitrator's terms of reference. If the parties decide to refer the dispute to an arbitrator (or arbitrators) jointly appointed by them, the conciliator (or the conciliation service) may help the parties to select an appropriate person. The law may also lay down certain formalities for referring a dispute to voluntary arbitration, and it will be a duty of the conciliator to see that the formalities are complied with.

In encouraging voluntary arbitration for the settlement of industrial disputes the legislation in many countries permits the reference of disputes to arbitration machinery set up and operated by the government at its own expense. It is often the government that has statutory responsibility for referring disputes to the arbitration machinery In such a situation, if both parties have agreed to arbitration the conciliator will recommend that the dispute be so referred.

PREVENTIVE CONCILIATION

12

Anywhere in the world, the government is concerned not only with the settlement of industrial disputes but also with their prevention. The idea of "preventing disputes" has been evolving and changing. At the beginning it mainly took the form of legislative regulation, with the object, in particular, of prohibiting or postponing strikes and lockouts. It was thought that "penalisation" would deter what the law defined as unlawful conduct. In addition the procedure of settlement itself was also relied upon as a means of preventing industrial action. When a conciliator succeeded in settling a dispute, he would also have shortened its duration, and perhaps prevented the parties from engaging in a costly and damaging trial of strength.

It is now widely accepted, however, that the prevention of disputes requires a positive and more varied approach. This view was recognised by the International Labour Conference when at its 36th Session, in 1953, it adopted a number of observations and conclusions regarding the organisation and working of national labour departments. With regard to the duties of labour departments in the fields of industrial relations and conditions of employment, the Conference made the following comments :

> Duties in these fields may include promoting collective bargaining, assisting in all matters pertaining to conciliation and arbitration and dealing with other aspects of wage fixing... These duties also imply positive action to increase co-operation and constructive relations in industry with the objective of attaining industrial peace and a high level of productivity.
>
> . . . .
>
> Assistance may also be provided, as requested, to employers' and workers' organisations in appropriate ways and without prejudice to their independence.[1]

Note may also be taken of certain observations regarding government services for the improvement of labour-management relations and settlement

---

[1] *Official Bulletin* (Geneva, ILO), Vol. XXXVI, No. 3, 31 Aug. 1953, p. 67, para. 7 (b).

of disputes which were adopted by the Fifth Asian Regional Conference of the ILO. They read in part as follows :

17. As part of a programme of positive action to promote constructive relations and co-operation in industry, the government may, in consultation with workers' and employers' organisations, consider the possibility of establishing and developing services to provide information, advice and assistance to the parties concerned on specific problems they have to deal with.

18. With regard to problems of day-to-day relations, the conciliation service may, on request, provide information, advice and asistance to both of the parties concerned so as to reduce existing or possible causes of friction, to prevent disputes from arising in the future and to develop better understanding between them for the long-term development of their relationship. This work may be entrusted to qualified conciliation or industrial relations officers who have been specially trained for the purpose.[1]

There are differences in the scope and nature of the activities in which national conciliation services now engage in order to prevent industrial disputes and promote constructive relations and co-operation between employers and workers. For the purposes of this guide all such activities, as distinct from activities directly concerned with the settlement of disputes, are considered under the heading of preventive conciliation. Two types of preventive activities are discussed below, namely the post-conciliation activities carried out by a conciliator and activities of a more general and largely promotional character.

POST-CONCILIATION PREVENTIVE ACTION

Not infrequently the conciliator dealing with a dispute finds that relations between the parties are strained, and that this fact may have a bearing, direct or indirect, on the issues. He may learn of these difficulties from his efforts to obtain details about the background and causes of the dispute or from the information which the parties volunteer to give him. In many cases a trained conciliator is in a position to help the parties in removing or finding appropriate remedies for the difficulties. He will want to do so especially if the difficulties will be a serious handicap to the parties' future relations.

For certain reasons, however, the conciliator cannot offer his help during the conciliation proceedings. First, by bringing in the question of these difficulties he would be introducing a new subject into the discussions ; there is a very real danger that in the tense atmosphere of the negotiations such a

---

[1] ILO : *Record of proceedings,* Fifth Asian Regional Conference, Melbourne, 1962, Appendix VII, pp. 193-195; also reproduced in ILO : *Government services for the improvement of labour-management relations and settlement of disputes in Asia,* An account of the work of the Labour-Management Relations Committee, Fifth Asian Regional Conference, Melbourne, 1962 (Geneva, Labour-Management Relations Series, No. 16 ; mimeographed), p. 119.

new subject would become a further bone of contention and would thus make it more difficult to settle the dispute. Secondly, the conciliator should concentrate on his efforts to settle the dispute, and should not have his attention distracted by another matter of substance that requires careful study and thoughtful consideration. In the third place the discussion of the difficulties can be more fruitful if it is carried out in a spirit of genuine objectivity and calm deliberation, which may be difficult to achieve during conciliation proceedings.

It will be seen that through this type of preventive activity, undertaken by him after a dispute has been terminated, a conciliator will actually be following up his previous intervention. A conciliator does not make an attempt at preventive conciliation after every dispute in which he has intervened, but only in those cases in which he finds he would be meeting a real need. As a rule it should be undertaken only in cases in which he has succeeded in bringing about a settlement ; if he failed, the parties will not think much of his ability to help them in other ways.

There is a further condition before a conciliator can engage in this type of preventive conciliation : it must be a recognised part of the activities of the national conciliation service. For the initiation, development and implementation of a preventive conciliation programme, the views and co-operation of employers' and workers' organisations are essential. Consequently only the national conciliation service, not a regional office or an individual conciliator, is in a position to undertake a programme of such activities : in undertaking preventive conciliation, a conciliator would be following principles established by the conciliation service and instructions issued by it.

Problems dealt with

The difficulties to which this type of preventive activity may be applied are essentially those arising from day-to-day relations. It can be particularly useful in helping the management and workers of an undertaking to remove or reduce the causes of friction and workers' dissatisfaction. The trouble may relate to the operation of an incentive pay system or a job evaluation scheme, or it may be due to weakness in the system of two-way communication or in methods of supervision. The parties may be experiencing difficulties in the administration and application of the current collective agreement, and there may be grounds for supposing that similar difficulties will occur after the conclusion of a new agreement.

The question of grievances seems to be one of the leading clues to the relations between the workers and the management in a specific company. The number of unresolved grievances over a certain period has definite implications. Numerous grievances could spell poor personnel policies ; they could also indicate a very heated situation which might presage an open conflict. On the other hand they may indicate that grievance machinery is working poorly or that union officers are inexperienced. The subjects of grievances provide another valuable lead to the source of trouble : if a number of grievances centre on a single provision of an agreement, there may be a misunderstanding by the management in applying the provision, or a member of a grievance committee may not fully understand management's right under that section of the agreement.

Much too often a limited number of disputes is management's benchmark for assuming the existence of sound working relations with its employees, whereas a glimpse behind the scenes may expose tyrannical foremen who threaten workers with unsavoury assignments or other prejudicial action if any opposition is expressed to their orders. Fear of retribution is a strong barrier that only a strong individual, or group of strong individuals, may seek to overcome ; but the lid cannot be kept for ever on such a state of affairs, and it can break out in an unauthorised strike at any time.

Procedures and methods of action

The manner in which post-conciliation preventive action is taken is a matter of national practice. A conciliator may handle a preventive conciliation case on the basis of a formal assignment, like an assignment to a dispute conciliation case. If, for example, the parties are faced with serious problems and the conciliator will need a series of meetings with them, he may be given a formal assignment, and he will then seek to develop with the parties a plan or programme to follow. On other occasions preventive conciliation may be carried out without a formal assignment, usually in the form of suggestions or advice conveyed by the conciliator to one or both of the parties through informal personal contacts instead of meetings.

Preventive conciliation may be directed at a specific difficulty, but when the parties agree to sit down with the conciliator to solve a particular problem they may be led to examine other difficulties as well. In complicated cases there will be various causes of bad relations in the plant, and more extended efforts may be needed to deal with the disruptive factors. Accordingly the conciliator may propose setting up a permanent joint committee. Depending on its terms of reference, it may be virtually fully engaged in a study and critical analysis of human relations in the company. The purposes of the committee will be defeated if the members bring to it the same attitude as they do to a joint conference in the course of collective bargaining. Strong guidance by the conciliator may thus be required : he may either draw up the "ground rules" for the committee or sit as committee chairman until the parties can make the committee function as a joint, co-operative effort.

When the difficulties relate to the application of a collective agreement, various types of remedial action are possible. When the difficulties are due to the absence of a grievance procedure, the conciliator's discussions with the parties may lead to an agreed procedure suitable to the needs of the undertaking. On the other hand, there may be already an existing agreed procedure that is not working well ; the problem then is to find out what changes can be made to improve its operation. It may be that the existing agreed procedure was soundly conceived but does not work well because the supervisors and trade union representatives who participate in the initial stages of the procedure are inexperienced ; with the help of the conciliator the parties may agree on a training programme on grievance adjustment for both supervisors and trade union personnel.

Finally, a conciliator can serve as a consultant or adviser to the parties in regard to problems that may arise under the conciliation settlement or a newly concluded collective agreement. The parties are, of course, not likely to make use of his services as a consultant if they are big employers or big organisations. However, many small or even medium-sized firms are not able to hire personnel specialists, and there are unions that cannot employ a permanent technical staff. For these firms and trade unions the services of a conciliator as a consultant or adviser may be welcome and can be a great help.

PROMOTIONAL ACTIVITIES

There is a certain analogy between the health of an individual and the health of industry.

In the case of industry not all disputes can be regarded as analogous to the diseases to which human beings are exposed. Disputes can arise from honest differences of view, and they can have a healthy therapeutic effect on the parties ; but disputes have also often occurred that need not have arisen or could have been easily prevented. The frequent occurrence of such disputes in an industry, and of the work stoppages that may accompany them, is certainly a sign that labour relations in it are not good. There are many other symptoms of bad relations that are much less dramatic and are therefore often ignored, such as poor employee performance and low labour productivity ; high labour turnover and widespread absenteeism and lateness in reporting for work ; numerous workers' grievances and disciplinary proceedings ; high accident and material wastage rates ; and restrictive and go-slow practices.

Preventive medicine is essentially aimed at promoting good health and the building up of the body's defences against disease. In industry good labour relations can be said to be the best defence against industrial disputes : good

125

relations are the best means of avoiding disputes altogether, or of reducing them to the smallest possible proportions. Preventive conciliation is essentially aimed at promoting good labour relations in industry, just as preventive medicine is essentially aimed at promoting good health in an individual.

Sound labour relations between particular parties are generally not established in a day. Nor does the existence of such relations mean that there will be no honest differences of view or conflicts of interests between the parties ; but it does imply that they have become capable of resolving their problems effectively by joint discussion, and it is therefore likely that when problems arise they will be able to find mutually satisfactory solutions to most of them.

A national conciliation service will generally have a programme for the promotion of good labour relations. In developing countries the programme will in many cases be of a rather limited character, the basic reason usually being lack of funds ; when government resources are scarce, investment in good labour relations is not usually given high priority. The discussion below is based on the practices in a number of countries. Its purpose its to show the varied types of activities that can be included in a programme to promote good labour relations, and the scope that such a programme can attain anywhere in due course.

Specific objectives

The programme of a national conciliation service for promoting good labour relations needs to have specific objectives. In most countries some of these objectives will be based on legislation while others will be a matter of administrative policy. In some countries certain objectives will be derived from decisions or instruments, such as industrial relations charters or voluntary codes of principles of labour-management relations, that have been adopted by tripartite advisory bodies.

As a matter of legislative policy one of the most important functions of the conciliation service in many countries is the encouragement and promotion of collective bargaining. This objective will include the development of joint negotiation machinery for general purposes, in addition to agreed machinery for dealing with grievances and disputes. It may also include the development of understandings and skills on the part of management and trade union representatives for the effective use of these procedures.

Among the objectives which the conciliation service may pursue in promoting good labour relations is the development of consultation and co-operation between employers and workers and their respective organisations. This objective may include the establishment of joint consultation machinery at the level of the undertaking, as well as at the industrial and national levels.

Another important objective is the development of sound personnel policies and practices within undertakings, especially for the benefit of small and medium-sized enterprises that cannot afford to set up personnel departments or to employ personnel management specialists.

In general, the conciliation service can promote the development of labour relations practices which experience has shown to be desirable or productive of satisfactory results. Very often such practices may involve unimportant matters or small details in day-to-day relations, but their cumulative effect in the long run can be very wholesome.

To achieve its objectives the conciliation service can employ various methods. These may include the provision of advice and assistance, the collection and dissemination of information and educational and training programmes.

Advice and assistance

The services of conciliators or industrial relations officers may be made available, on request, to interested parties to lend advice or assistance in various matters. In principle, however, this work should be entrusted only to officials who have been specially trained for the purpose.

They may, for example, advise or assist in setting up joint negotiation machinery, agreed machinery for adjusting grievances or for settling disputes, machinery for labour-management co-operation or joint consultation. They can advise on the essential preparatory steps to be taken for the establishment of a grievance procedure or of joint consultation machinery within the undertaking. It is not enough, however, for the parties to agree on setting up any particular machinery ; it is also essential that the machinery should be made to work effectively in practice. For this purpose the advice and assistance of trained conciliation or industrial relations officers can be very helpful.

Their services can also be made available to help the parties in an advisory capacity either for the long-range development of their relations or to deal with any specific problem or difficulty. This work differs from the post-conciliation preventive activity of a conciliator in that there is no immediate background of dispute between the parties.

Another field in which the advice and assistance of conciliators or industrial relations officers can be of great help in the promotion of good labour relations is the development of sound personnel policies and practices. Among the problems which may require particular attention are the development of two-way communication and labour discipline, including dismissal procedures.

The development of informal contact between conciliators and leading employers and trade unionists with whom they are likely to have dealings in the course of their duties plays an important role in preventive conciliation. (The conduct of conciliation proceedings can also be greatly eased if those concerned are on friendly terms, although the value of this should not be over-estimated when important issues are at stake.) It is therefore useful if a conciliator can avail himself of opportunities of meeting employers' and trade union representatives at social functions, conferences, training courses and similar occasions. It sometimes happens that at meetings of this kind a conciliator is asked informally for his advice or opinion on possible developments at an early stage in a situation in which a dispute might arise ; by giving guidance at that stage he may succeed in putting the matter on a course leading to an agreed solution.

Collection and dissemination of information

The role of the conciliation service in assembling and analysing information and making it available to individual members of its staff was described in Chapter 4. Good labour relations can also be promoted by making information available to outsiders as well. For one thing, it is important for the service to be able to provide substantial information in answering written inquiries from interested parties. More generally, it can bring useful information to the attention of management, trade unions and employers' organisations through publications and other communications media. It may be emphasised that the collection and analysis of information is also important for the field work of industrial relations officers and for the educational and training programmes in which the conciliation service may be engaged or participating.

For the promotion of collective bargaining it may be useful for the conciliation service to prepare model agreements on trade union recognition or on the establishment of joint negotiation machinery, grievance machinery or voluntary conciliation and arbitration machinery. If the conciliation service has made a compilation of existing collective agreements in the country, it can be made available for consultation by parties that are in the process of negotiating agreements, and analyses of the contents of such agreements can also be made available for publication.

For the promotion of consultation and co-operation the service can prepare model constitutions for joint consultation machinery ; such models will correspond to different sets of purposes, conditions and needs. The service can also publish information on the progress made in the establishment of such machinery, and on its practical achievements and results as regards particular parties, in addition to studies on such subjects as relatively successful experiments. Depending on the objectives of the conciliation service, work in this field can be extended to the participation of workers in decisions within undertakings.

The field of labour relations is extremely wide and it is not possible to enumerate all the subjects in regard to which information may be disseminated, but they will include specific aspects of personnel management and labour relations within undertakings, including programmes to increase productivity, wage incentive and job evaluation schemes, and generally factors that hinder or promote good relations.

To acquire more information that it can usefully disseminate, the conciliation service may encourage and assist studies and research on the part of research and academic institutions. Thus the results of research elsewhere can be passed on by the service to employers and trade unions throughout the country.

As regards the form of publications, the conciliation service can make use of those regularly issued by the ministry or department of labour. It can also issue its own publications devoted exclusively to labour relations subjects, as well as monographs or special studies.

Educational and training programmes

Educational and training programmes have a fundamental role to play in the development of good relations between employers and workers in developing countries. They can help to overcome the handicaps due to the lack or inadequacy of experience on the part of management and trade union representatives who perform labour relations functions. On the one hand, training programmes can increase their skill in handling the procedural side of the conduct of joint negotiations and the use of grievance or joint consultation machinery, while on the other hand programmes of a broadly educational character can increase their understanding of the problems that are the subject of collective bargaining, grievance adjustment or joint consultation.

Where resources permit, the conciliation service, in co-operation with employers' and workers' organisations, can organise short-term training courses or seminars for management and trade union representatives. It can also encourage and assist employers' and workers' organisations in their own training programmes.

APPENDIX: ADVICE FOR CONCILIATORS

The following is a summary of the advice that can be given to conciliators on the basis of the present guide.

Basic attitude and approach

The conciliator should always maintain a strictly impartial and neutral attitude towards the two parties. No word, sign or gesture on his part should show that he favours one party.

He should always remember that his function requires a full independence of judgement. He should not allow himself to be swayed by any external pressure or influence, either from the parties or from any other quarter.

The parties may accept his intervention simply because he offers his services to them on behalf of the government or under government authority, and he should not automatically assume that they regard him as a conciliator capable of helping them resolve their dispute. He will have to establish his acceptability to the parties : he will have to make them believe that he is capable and that he sincerely desires to help them. He can establish this belief not so much by the words he uses as by his attitude, by his actions and by the substance of what he says.

He must take the view that the dispute constitutes an important problem for the parties and requires the best of his efforts : on no account must he deal with it as if it were just a routine matter, or with an air of bureaucratic complacency.

He should make the fullest preparations for the case; obtain as full information as possible about the background and circumstances of the dispute and about any unfamiliar persons with whom he will be dealing; and be fully informed about the subject matter of the issues in dispute.

Meetings

The conciliator is a servant of the parties. In matters of scheduling and arranging meetings he should spare no effort to meet their wishes.

He should not schedule a meeting unless he has a clear idea of what he hopes to achieve by it ; otherwise he may just be wasting the time and attention of the parties. He should select the type of meetings—joint or separate or a combination of the two—that best suit his objectives at that stage of the negotiations. He should prepare himself fully for every meeting ; in particular he should read over and carefully study his notes on the previous meetings, especially the last one. He should excuse himself from attending any party that evening, and should instead do his homework for the meeting on the next day, where he will need a clear head. Before going to the meeting he should make sure that his case folder is in order.

While expecting the parties to be punctual, he should make sure of arriving before they do.

He should extend his greetings and welcome not only to the leading or principal members of each side's negotiating committee but to every member of it.

As chairman of a joint meeting the conciliator is obviously a person of importance, but he must not let that fact go to his head, and must not try to conduct the meeting as if he were holding court. He should be rather informal, while retaining the dignity of his position. He will not be in any danger of losing his dignity by being friendly. One can still be dignified in shirt sleeves if the weather is very hot and there is no air conditioning.

As chairman of a joint meeting the conciliator's job is to maintain order and encourage rational and constructive discussion. The parties should be allowed to carry on the discussion with as little interruption from the conciliator as possible : the less he says the better.

He should never on any account criticise a party at a joint meeting or in the presence of the other. To do so is the easiest way to destroy the parties' belief in his impartiality. Neither party would like to be placed in an embarrassing position, particularly by the conciliator. In a joint meeting, he should not do or say anything that will, in effect, strengthen the position of one party on a particular issue.

If he has views on the merits of either party's position on the issues, or on the soundness of any proposition or the correctness or adequacy of any information submitted by either party, he should hold them in reserve for a separate meeting with the party concerned. If he feels it necessary to criticise unreasonable behaviour on the part of certain negotiators, he should do so only at a separate meeting and only if he is on good terms with them personally and if he is certain that they will not take offence. He should not criticise one party before the other in a separate meeting.

If he does not understand a certain point, he should ask for clarification, and should continue to ask if he is still not clear about what one of the parties is driving at. He should not hesitate to do so out of fear that the parties may think he is not very clever ; the situation would be more serious if he were ultimately to make a suggestion which showed that he had missed their point.

The conciliator should not give the parties the impression that he is trying to hurry them ; usually they do not like it.

The search for agreement

First of all, the conciliator must obtain a clear idea of the parties' positions and of the extent of the differences that separate them. If there are a number of issues, he should find out the parties' real stand on each of them (What are the relative priorities they attach to each issue? Which issues, if any, are only bargaining points or throw-away items ?).

If he has to persuade either party to change its position, or to modify, reduce or withdraw a demand or counter-proposal, he should do so at a separate meeting. Even in a separate meeting with one party, he should not allow himself to be drawn into endorsing that party's position.

He should not take any positive initiative, like suggesting a possible solution, as long as the parties are bent on justifying their respective positions. Before taking such an initiative, he needs to be sure that the parties are in a mood to consider it. He should seek to induce such a mood.

He should make sure that every aspect of each issue, including possible underlying motives, is fully explored. He should see to it that neither party has any misunderstanding or misconception of the other's position.

He should make sure that both sides fully understand the consequences of a deadlock. He should do all he can to encourage the parties to offer proposed solutions in the form of modified proposals and counter-proposals.

He should always remember that he is not the judge of the parties but their assistant in reaching agreement.

He should be fully prepared to offer one or more possible solutions to each of the issues in dispute. He should carefully consider his timing in offering a possible alternative solution. When he wishes to offer an alternative solution he should do so by exploring it with either party at a separate meeting. If the party with which he discusses it first accepts it as presented by him or in an amended version, the conciliator should use his good judgement as to whether he should encourage that party to present the agreed version at a joint meeting, or whether he should discuss it with the second party as his own suggestion or as proposal from the other party.

The conciliator needs to be patient in his endeavours. He should not expect the parties to change their minds easily or that agreement will be easily reached.

He should not himself make a proposal for settling the dispute as a whole unless he has exhausted all possibilities of obtaining a settlement on the basis of the parties' proposed solutions. If the dispute involves a number of issues, his proposal should be for a "package" settlement that will dispose of all such issues. He should not formally make his proposal at a joint meeting without having first obtained the agreement of each of the parties separately.

If it is not possible to obtain agreement on the issues, he should do his best to persuade the parties to agree to submit the dispute to binding arbitration or to another procedure for peacefully settling it as early as possible.

MINIONS

BANANA!

Art by: Renau   Windsor and Maidenhead   **AH-KOON**

Find the Minion taking photos!

PAF

050

Renaud + Didier 2014

035

RENAUD + DIDIER 2014

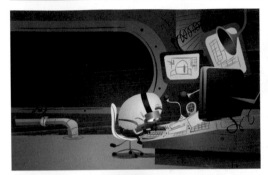

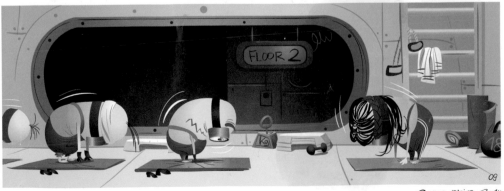

REVAUD + DIDIER 2014

PERFECT TARGET!

RENAUD + DIDIER 2014

FOR 3 POINTS!

RENAUD + DIDIER 2014

RENAUD + DIDIER 2014

08

RENAUD + DIDIER 2014

03

RENAUD + DIDIER 2014

BURNOUT

10

REVAUD + DIDIER 2014

045

REVAUD + DIDIER 2014

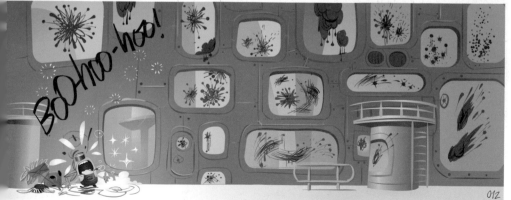

RENAUD + DIDIER 2014

TEST: WATERMELON

RENAUD + DIDIER 201

REVAUD + DIDIER 2014

11

REVAUD + DIDIER 2014

REVAUD + DIDIER 2014

FRESH PAINT

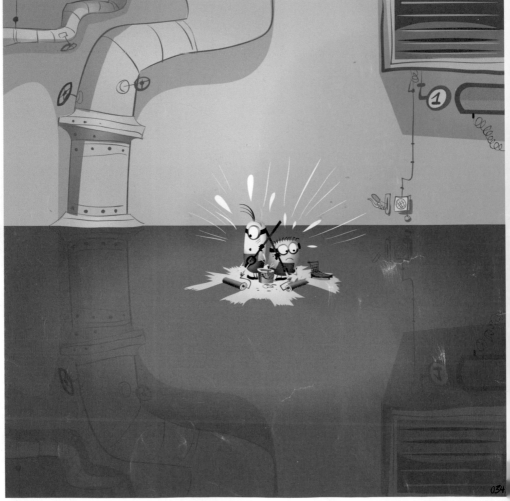

034

RENAUD + DIDIER 2014

REVAUD + DIDIER 2014

REVAUD + DIDIER 2014

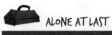

RENAUD + DIDIER 2014

HE WHO LAUGHS LAST LAUGHS BEST...

017

RENAUD + DIDIER 2014

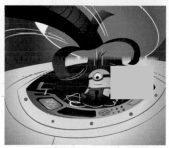
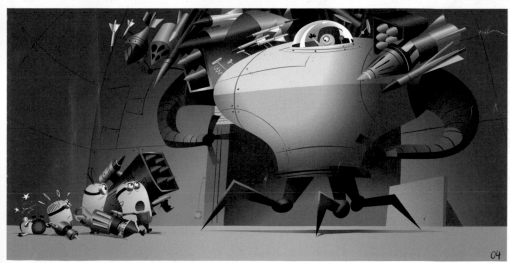

04

RENAUD + DIDIER 2014

The next day...

RENAUD + DIDIER 2014

REVAUD + DIDIER 2014

FRUIT FRUSTRATION

RENAUD + DIDIER 2014

BANANA DREAM

REVAUD + DIDIER 2014

S.O.S. MINIONS

025

RENAUD + DIDIER 2014

RENAUD + DIDIER 2014

REVAUD + DIDIER 201

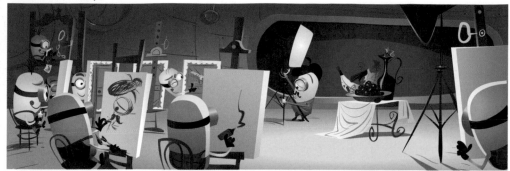

014

RENAUD + DIDIER 2014

 **TEMPTATION**

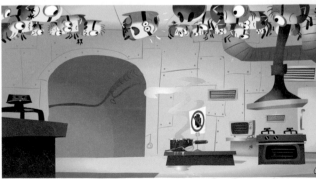

RENAUD + DIDIER 20j

REVAUD + DIDIER 2014

Revaud + Didier 2014

RÉVAUD + DIDIER 2014

RECYCLING

026

RENAUD + DIDIER 2014

The next day...

037

REVAUD + DIDIER 2014

JOKER...

RENAUD + DIDIER 2014

REVAUD + DiDiER 2014

RENAUD + DIDIER 201

SAFETY ABOVE ALL!

RENAUD + DIDIER 2014

RENAUD + DIDIER 20

ZZZZ ELECTRIC BALLET

046

RENAUD + DIDIER 2014

03

RENAUD + DIDIER 20.